D0253025

the little book of
self-care

200 Ways to Refresh, Restore, and Rejuvenate

Adams Media

New York London Toronto Sydney New Delhi

Adams Media
An Imprint of Simon & Schuster, Inc.
57 Littlefield Street
Avon, Massachusetts 02322

Copyright © 2017 by Simon & Schuster, Inc.

All rights reserved, including the right to reproduce this book or portions thereof in any form whatsoever. For information address Adams Media Subsidiary Rights Department, 1230 Avenue of the Americas, New York, NY 10020.

First Adams Media hardcover edition OCTOBER 2017

ADAMS MEDIA and colophon are trademarks of Simon and Schuster.

For information about special discounts for bulk purchases, please contact Simon & Schuster Special Sales at 1-866-506-1949 or business@simonandschuster.com.

The Simon & Schuster Speakers Bureau can bring authors to your live event. For more information or to book an event contact the Simon & Schuster Speakers Bureau at 1-866-248-3049 or visit our website at www.simonspeakers.com.

Interior design by Colleen Cunningham

Manufactured in the United States of America

10 9 8 7

Library of Congress Cataloging-in-Publication Data
Adams Media, author.
The little book of self-care
Avon, Massachusetts: Adams Media, 2017.
LCCN 2017020005 | ISBN 9781507204917 (hc) | ISBN 9781507204924 (ebook)
LCSH: Relaxation. | Stress management. | Mind and body. | Self-care, Health.
LCC RA785 .L58 2017 | DDC 613.7/92--dc23
LC record available at https://lccn.loc.gov/2017020005

ISBN 978-1-5072-0491-7
ISBN 978-1-5072-0492-4 (ebook)

Many of the designations used by manufacturers and sellers to distinguish their products are claimed as trademarks. Where those designations appear in this book and Simon & Schuster, Inc., was aware of a trademark claim, the designations have been printed with initial capital letters.

This book is intended as general information only, and should not be used to diagnose or treat any health condition. In light of the complex, individual, and specific nature of health problems, this book is not intended to replace professional medical advice. The ideas, procedures, and suggestions in this book are intended to supplement, not replace, the advice of a trained medical professional. Consult your physician before adopting any of the suggestions in this book, as well as about any condition that may require diagnosis or medical attention. The author and publisher disclaim any liability arising directly or indirectly from the use of this book.

Contains material adapted from the titles listed at the end of this book.

contents

body   15

mind   71

spirit 127

surroundings

*introduction

Self-care—it's something all of us need more of but few of us make time for in our busy lives. *The Little Book of Self-Care* is here to change that. In it you'll find quick, simple ways to quiet the noise around you, reduce everyday stresses, and remind yourself of the many blessings in your life. You deserve to take time to relax, refresh, and rejuvenate your body, mind, and spirit to maximize your full potential.

Think about the last time you did something to take care of yourself. If you're drawing a blank, do something about it right now. Open to any page and start taking care of yourself the way you take care of so many other people and things in your life.

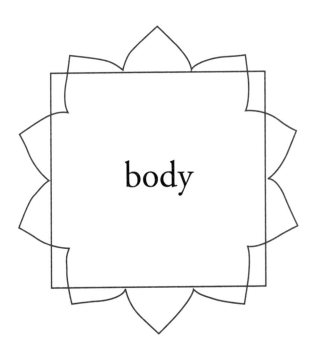

body

Try a Hot Stone Massage

If you've never had a hot stone massage, you are in for a one-of-a-kind experience. The stones are used in two different ways during the massage. One way is by applying heat to areas of the body to make the muscles relax and increase blood flow to speed up healing. Hot stones are usually placed along the length of the spine or at the chakra centers of your body. A towel will be between you and the stones, so don't worry about being burned. Another way the stones are used is as tools for deep tissue massage. Your massage therapist will cover the warm, smooth stones in oil and rub them on your body using long strokes in the area she is working on. This is an unbelievable sensation and one you will truly enjoy. If you are used to traditional Swedish massage, try this version instead.

Moisturize with Warm Lotion

Stepping out of a hot shower into a cold bathroom can feel quite unpleasant. Why give yourself more goose bumps with cold lotion? Heat up the lotion ahead of time and you'll be in for a delightful treat. You don't need to use the oven or microwave to do this; just keep the bottle of lotion near or on your radiator or heating vent during the winter. The warm lotion will feel luxurious on your body.

Eat Organic

Eating food without pesticides, hormones, and fertilizers is better for your body and for the earth. Organic food has become increasingly popular in the past ten to twenty years, as people are becoming more conscious of what they feed themselves and their families. Visit a grocery store that sells organic products, like Whole Foods or Trader Joe's, and do your weekly grocery shopping. Organic food tends to cost a few dollars more, but it is worth it. You know what you're putting into your body, and you don't have to worry about anything unnatural.

Get a Good Night's Sleep

Sleep is absolutely necessary for a healthy mind and body, yet many people don't get enough. Sure, you may unwind from work and have some fun, but if you don't get enough sleep, you are making yourself vulnerable to stress and illness. Spend some time modifying your sleeping habits if sleep is a problem for you. Set a bedtime, and stick to it. Keep technology out of your bedroom. Don't eat or drink right before bed. Limit (or eliminate) your intake of nicotine, alcohol, and caffeine. If you still have trouble sleeping despite changing your habits, visit with a healthcare professional, as sleep disorders are common but serious conditions.

Take a Morning Walk

Start your day off right with a brisk thirty-minute walk. Early in the morning, before everyone is awake and the sun is just starting to rise, is the best time. Many people find it to be the most spiritual part of the day. Take this time to meditate and prepare for the day ahead. It's a great way to allow your mind to relax, and not only will you feel refreshed and centered, but you will also find that you have more energy throughout the day. Listen to some soothing music, or if you want to get your blood flowing, bring some dance or techno music. It has also been shown that if you have a difficult time exercising consistently, doing so in the morning will make it easier to develop a routine. Make sure to eat a healthy breakfast when you return from your walk.

Practice a Variety of Stretches

Websites, *YouTube* videos, exercise books, and personal trainers offer differing advice on what stretch to do, how long to hold a stretch, how often you need to stretch, and so on. Every person is different, and you should follow advice that is personalized for your body. What is important is that you take the time to lengthen your muscles in some way. It helps to know the four types of stretches:

1. **ACTIVE:** Usually used before a training session. You can take almost any stretch and make it active by moving in and out of the stretch using your breath.
2. **DYNAMIC:** Involves momentum and muscular effort in order to move primary joints that are going to be used during activity. Big shoulder circles, leg swings, hip circles, and standing spinal rotations are all dynamic stretches.
3. **PASSIVE:** A relaxing, cooling, and calming type of stretch. They do not require you to hold your body weight and are mostly done in a seated or lying down position.
4. **STATIC:** Has no movement involved but muscles are recruited to hold the position, such as the yoga Downward Facing Dog pose.

Make Homemade Fruit Popsicles

Popsicles are a favorite summertime treat, but they are usually made with high fructose corn syrup and water. Instead, make your own popsicles using 100 percent fruit juice. Fill an ice cube tray with your favorite juice. Cover the tray with two or three layers of aluminum foil, and poke wooden sticks through the foil into each individual tray square (you can find sticks at your local craft store). Place the tray in the freezer, and wait until they are fully frozen. In a few hours you'll have a delicious snack that is good for you. Try using exotic fruit juices, like mango or guava. You can't always find these types of popsicles in the store, and if you serve them at a barbecue, you'll definitely impress your guests. Enjoy this guiltless snack today!

Let Someone Brush Your Hair

You brush your hair every day, but it's a completely different experience when someone else does it for you. Ask a friend or partner to brush your hair. Have her use a large paddle brush so it makes your hair very soft. If she does it slowly and softly, it may be enough to put you to sleep. Offer to return the favor; even if she has short hair, she is sure to enjoy this wonderful sensation.

Make Your Own Body Oil

Using body oil is a fabulous after-shower treat to keep your skin moist and smooth. Just like any bath product, body oil can be pricey. You need only three ingredients to make your own, so why not? Natural beauty products are better for you and the earth. You will need:

* Grape-seed or sunflower oil
* Fragrant essential oil of your choice
* A small bottle

You can get essential oil at your local holistic or metaphysical shop, and you might be able to find it at a health food shop. Do a test to make sure you aren't allergic to the oil before you make your batch. Fill the bottle ⅔ of the way with the grape-seed or sunflower oil. Then put in drops of the essential oil until the fragrance is strong enough for you. This will be different for everyone, so add it drop by drop. Shake the bottle well. Your body oil should stay fresh for six to twelve months. Body oil is great for people with dry skin, so make some for friends and family as well.

Increase Your Fiber Intake with a Fig Smoothie

If you've tried fresh figs, you know how delightful they can be. Plus, figs are high in potassium, which is important for lowering high blood pressure (hypertension). If you have a masticating juicer, use a wider mesh net attachment to allow some fiber through. Alternatively, for a thicker smoothie, process the figs in a blender to purée, then add to the juice. To make the smoothie, gather these ingredients:

* 10 figs, halved
* 3 medium carrots, trimmed
* 1 small sugar beet, greens optional
* 2 stalks celery, with leaves
* 2 medium apples, cored
* 1 cucumber, sliced
* ½ lemon, peeled

Process the figs in a masticating juicer or blender until smooth. Process the carrots and beets through an electronic juicer according to the manufacturer's directions. Add the celery, apples, and cucumber to the juicer, followed by the lemon. Whisk or blend the ingredients together and enjoy! Yields 1½ cups.

Exercise for Thirty Minutes a Day

Regular exercise is essential for your physical health and to preserve your mental acuity. Aerobic exercise helps get the blood coursing through your system, carrying oxygen and glucose to your brain—two substances the brain needs in order to function. The US federal guidelines for exercise say that getting at least thirty minutes a day most days a week will help prevent heart disease, osteoporosis, diabetes, obesity, and now, perhaps, Alzheimer's. If you do nothing else, a brisk thirty-minute walk every day will do wonders for your brain health.

Treat Headaches with Herbal Remedies

Seven in ten Americans have at least one headache a year, and 45 million people live with chronic headaches. Instead of automatically reaching for over-the-counter pills the next time you get one, consider an herbal option:

* **BUTTERBUR:** Extracts from this shrub have analgesic, anti-inflammatory, and antiseizure actions. In several recent studies, they produced a marked decrease in the severity and frequency of migraines.
* **CAYENNE:** Applied topically, cayenne preparations have been shown to relieve and even prevent the devastating pain of cluster headaches.
* **FEVERFEW:** This is perhaps the best-known herbal headache remedy. It has been shown in several studies to reduce the frequency of migraine attacks—and limit their symptoms when they do occur.
* **LAVENDER:** The essential oil of this flowering plant has been used effectively to treat several types of headache pain. The same is true of peppermint oil.
* **WILLOW:** The salicin from the bark of this tree is a potent analgesic. Its headache-fighting properties are well proven in both laboratory and clinical studies.

Check Your Body Composition

Your body composition refers to the percentage of fat and percentage of fat-free body mass that makes up your total body weight. Fat-free mass, also known as lean-body mass, consists primarily of muscle tissue, bones, and blood—essentially, all the rest of your body that is not fat.

Research suggests that the ideal percentage of body fat for men is 15 to 18 percent. For women, the ideal range of body fat is 22 to 25 percent. (These are just suggested ranges! Ask your doctor what's right for you.) When you begin an exercise program, you might want to measure your body composition. This way, you'll have a baseline against which to measure the effectiveness of your program over time. If you're a person who is motivated by numbers, this is a concrete way to stay excited about your progress. There are multiple methods for determining your body composition. You can find body fat calculators on many health-oriented websites. You can also be weighed underwater or measured with skin calipers, or obtain the information through other methods available at health clubs or health clinics.

Get Enough Calcium

Calcium is an important part of a balanced diet because it helps strengthen bones, helps regulate your blood pressure, helps secrete hormones and digestive enzymes, assists directly with weight loss, regulates heart muscle function, and helps boost your metabolism. The easiest way to stock up on your calcium needs is by eating dairy products like milk, cheese, and yogurt. But there are many other foods that are also rich in calcium: dark green leafy vegetables like broccoli, spinach, kale, and collards; fish with edible bones; calcium-fortified soy milk; tofu made with calcium; shelled almonds; turnips; mustard greens; sesame seeds; blackstrap molasses; calcium-fortified cereals; and calcium-fortified orange juice.

Eat More Superfoods

If you're looking for a great return on your nutritional investment, superfoods are the way to go. Superfoods are loaded with vitamins, minerals, and other great nutrients that help fight disease, boost metabolism, and make you feel great. All of these foods are unprocessed and reasonably easy to find, so unless you're allergic, go ahead and add them to your diet and enjoy the benefits. Superfoods include: avocado, beans, blueberries, broccoli, dark greens (like spinach), flax, oats, olive oil, oranges, pomegranate, pumpkin, salmon, soy, tea (green or black), tomatoes, turkey, walnuts, and yogurt.

Hire a Personal Trainer

A personal trainer is a pro who trains all types of people, from aspiring athletes to seventy-year-old grandmothers. A good personal trainer will first assess your fitness level and test you to see where your weak spots are, then will design a training program to correct any deficiencies and prepare you for your specific goal. The benefits of having a personal trainer include the one-on-one attention and instant feedback as you learn proper techniques. Your PT will be able to assess your limits and design a program that keeps you from overtraining. Most PTs will design workouts with some variety to keep you from being bored with your training while you work the same muscles with different workouts. Finally, a personal trainer can be your motivator. The PT will take pride in your progress and will naturally want to cheer you on.

Wear Sunscreen

Protect your skin from the harmful rays of the sun by wearing sunscreen. No matter what sun protection factor (SPF) it is, make sure to reapply at least two or three times during the day. Be especially careful during the midday hours, when the sun is at its strongest. Remember to apply sunscreen at home or in the car at least thirty minutes before sun exposure to maximize your protection. Sunscreens with UVA and UVB protection are most effective in preventing skin cancer and other skin ailments. If you don't like the oily feeling on your skin all day, look for an oil-free sunscreen. Allow your body to live a long and healthy life by protecting it when having fun in the sun!

Do a Quick At-Home Facial

After a long day, your face might ache from talking, eye-strain, or the elements. Place cool cucumber slices on your eyes after applying a facial mask or aftershave for an easy, inexpensive, in-home spa experience. Dim the lights, light some candles, lie down, and enjoy the cucumber's coolness sinking into your skin. Try slightly damp used tea bags, a chilled eye mask, or smooth stones as variations.

Cook at Home

Cooking is considered one of the ultimate forms of relaxation by a great many people. It puts the world behind us by putting us into a rhythm of following the directions, sticking to a precise schedule, and anticipating the delicious meal to come. Even if you're too busy to cook every night, try to set aside one night a week for some kitchen time.

Most of us love to try new dishes and eat at new restaurants to avoid getting bogged down with the same old thing night in and night out. But sometimes that results in forgetting our old favorites. Change up your schedule a bit by resolving to cook your favorite dish once in a while.

Your recipe can be for anything you want from any period in your life. Perhaps you're longing for a plate of the one-of-a-kind macaroni your mother used to make. Experimentation in the kitchen can be wonderful, but it doesn't have to be a new thing each and every night. The old favorites are just that for a reason.

Make an Appointment
for a Physical

The most important indulgence in life is to take care of your body. It is the only one you have, and you must take it for a yearly tune-up to ensure everything is working properly. Many people are nervous about doctors and therefore skip these crucial appointments; however, they should be looked at as "you" moments. If you are uncomfortable with your doctor, get a new one. You should feel 100 percent in control and completely comfortable with your doctor. You work hard for those benefits, and it is your right and responsibility to make sure your "temple" is well taken care of.

Try a New Class at Your Gym

Your local gym offers numerous classes, and almost everyone is too intimidated to join until they try it once. Sign up today and try one out. You will notice immediately that many people feel the same way you do and have difficulty with similar exercises. Working out in a group also keeps you motivated, and you will begin to make a group of new friends who are all working toward a common goal. Most gyms will allow you to sit in on a class and watch for a little bit to decide if that level is right for you. Make working out fun and enjoyable, and join a class today!

Encourage Weight Loss
with a Juice Blend

If you would like to lose a few pounds, you might want to eat more grapefruit. Adding grapefruit to your diet is believed to assist in weight loss through an enzyme that acts with protein to regulate insulin levels and control hunger pangs. One study funded by the Florida Department of Citrus found that the addition of a half grapefruit or 4 ounces of juice with meals resulted in an average weight loss of more than three pounds in twelve weeks, with some participants losing as much as ten pounds! Try this juice blend to incorporate grapefruit into your diet in a sweet and delicious way—and without adding refined sugar.

To make this Citrus-Blueberry Juice Blend, gather these ingredients:

* 1 cup blueberries
* 2 oranges, peeled
* 1 pink grapefruit, peeled

Process the fruits through an electronic juicer according to the manufacturer's directions. Drink as soon as possible after preparation. Yields 1 cup.

Get a Reiki Treatment

Reiki (pronounced "ray-key") is a Japanese stress reduction and relaxation technique that also promotes healing. Each of us has a life energy force (sometimes referred to as chi or qi) that can sometimes become low or blocked. When this happens, we are more likely to feel stressed out and sick. Reiki uses universal healing energy to remove these blockages and has the ability to heal mind, body, and spirit. A trained Reiki practitioner will lay her hands on or above you in various positions on your body to initiate the flow of healing energy. Practitioners can often feel where there is a blockage and may concentrate on a specific area longer than others. A normal session lasts about an hour. After a Reiki session, you will experience feelings of relaxation, peace, and well-being.

Take a Daily Vitamin

Many people don't get the vital nutrients they need from food alone. Taking a daily vitamin can assist you in living a long and healthy life. These vitamins help you release energy from the food you eat and build strong bones and tissue. Vitamins can be expensive, but it is a small price to pay when you think of how it is helping your body stay in tip-top shape. Consult with your doctor on what vitamin will be the best for your body and if it might interfere with any medication you are currently taking.

Learn Some Basic Yoga Poses

Yoga is an ancient Indian practice that has become very popular around the world for both physical and spiritual well-being. By using methods of breathing and postures, yoga is believed to improve overall health, reduce anxiety, promote relaxation and flexibility, and increase self-awareness. Almost all gyms and fitness centers now offer yoga classes to the public—sign up for one today. If you aren't familiar with yoga, try a beginner class like hatha yoga. You will practice breathing and do simple stretches and postures. Every yoga instructor will tell you not to do more than you are comfortable doing. Go at your own pace, and focus on matching your breath with the movements. You will come out feeling refreshed and centered.

Boost Your Immunity with Tea

Licorice and ginger are a good combo to remember during allergy season. Ginger has a warming, drying action on the upper respiratory tract, and licorice helps support your immune system. Amla has immune supporting properties of its own, and it also has a yummy flavor. Use powdered herbs for the easiest tea—just stir it all up and enjoy your Licorice, Amla, and Ginger Tea! Gather these ingredients:

* 1 tablespoon powdered licorice root
* 4 tablespoons powdered amla berries
* 3 tablespoons powdered ginger root

1. Blend together the powdered licorice root, amla berries, and ginger root and store them in an airtight container. Make sure to label your tea so you can find it easily when you need it.
2. To make a cup of tea, bring 8 ounces of water to a boil and add 1 teaspoon of the licorice, amla, and ginger blend. Allow to simmer for 10 minutes. Pour into your favorite mug. The licorice and amla have a sweet taste, so be sure to take a sip before you reach for your favorite sweetener. You may not need it. (Yields 24 servings.)

Eat Nutrient-Rich Vegetables

Fruits and vegetables are an obvious part of any health regimen because they are loaded with essential nutrients in their most natural and useful form—and the more fruits and vegetables you eat, the more satiated you will feel and you will be able to avoid high-calorie foods and fat. In fact, many vegetables will satisfy—or nearly satisfy—your daily requirements for several vitamins. From dark leafy greens rich in calcium, iron, and magnesium to the cruciferous vegetables like bok choy, broccoli, cabbage, turnips, and water cress that have cancer-preventing antioxidants to nutrient-rich vegetables like carrots, potatoes, yams, and tomatoes, vegetables are always a good thing to snack on and include with each meal. The majority of Americans don't consume nearly enough fruits and vegetables. Government health officials suggest a minimum of five servings of fruit and vegetables daily—twice the amount suggested for meat and dairy. Be sure you're getting enough!

Get Your Teeth Cleaned

Getting your teeth cleaned may seem anything but blissful, but taking care of your teeth is so important. We all seem to put off the dentist appointment for anything that comes up, but it should be one of our top priorities. Not only are your teeth part of your body and essential for digesting food, but they're also part of the image you present to the world—your smile. It can become very costly as you get older if you decide to let your teeth go and not get them cleaned every six months. To cut down on those bills and the worry about a potential problem, remember to take a few minutes out of every day to brush your teeth at least twice and floss.

Take a Nap

If your last nap was twenty to thirty years ago, take some time out today for a quick snooze. A thirty-minute midday nap has been proven to lessen stress, increase learning, and improve health. This may be hard if you are at work, but even closing your eyes for five minutes in your office is proven to relieve stress and give you a boost of energy. Those few moments will help you decompress and give your body the break it needs. Try to avoid napping for more than an hour, as you may have a hard time falling asleep that evening.

Make Time for a Quickie

Studies have shown that having sex can better your overall health and increase your life expectancy. A romp in the sheets twice a week can reduce the risk of heart disease, reduce depression, and improve bladder control and overall fitness. Isn't this enough of a reason to make time for a quickie? Even if you are too tired or too stressed, a quick ten- to fifteen-minute session can do the trick. It will definitely take the edge off a rough day and give you the quick jolt of energy you need to clean the dishes. Try it today, just before leaving for work or before dressing up for dinner tonight. Throw on your birthday suit and keep it quick!

Have an Acupuncture Treatment

Acupuncture is an ancient Chinese medical treatment that has been practiced for centuries. It involves inserting small, thin needles into different areas of the body and manipulating them for the purpose of relieving pain and stress. The areas of the body where the needles are placed follow the meridians where qi or chi, vital life-force energy, flows. People get acupuncture for a variety of health reasons, even as a fertility treatment. Find an acupuncturist in your area to get a treatment. Let him know where your pain is and what you would like to accomplish with acupuncture. Do some research before your first visit so you can ask questions.

Go on a Detox Diet

Detoxification diets are day-, week-, or month-long ventures to purge, purify, and replenish the body. The practice of purifying the body for health improvement, disease prevention, and even spiritual purification is a worldwide practice that is growing in popularity today. The focus is on detoxification, improved system functioning, and weight loss, with the ideal result being an optimized state of health in which you improve everything from breathing and digestion to thought processes and energy levels. There are many types of detoxes to choose from (juices, soups, whole foods, sugar-free, and so on)—ask your doctor if one is right for you.

Strengthen Your Core

You've likely seen *YouTube* videos, books, or DVDs that advertise strengthening your "core." It sounds like marketing hype, but your core is indeed very important to your physical health. Your body's core is essentially made up of the muscles of your trunk—the area between the shoulder "girdle" and the legs. This includes, of course, your abdominal muscles. Here's why it's so important: your core is essential to all body movement. Everything you do comes from your core. You can do most of the core-strengthening exercises in twenty minutes two times a week. Yoga and Pilates are both great for strengthening your core, but the simple pushup is also a great core-strengthening exercise you can do at home. Boxing, gymnastics, dancing, and basketball are other good core-strengthening activities. What's important to know is that time invested in strengthening your core will pay off big time—no matter what sport or workout you prefer.

Take a Long, Hot Bath

When was the last time you took a long, hot bath? If you can't remember, then it might be time to reconsider the idea of taking one as a way of distancing yourself from a long day and relaxing enough to think about getting to bed in decent time. Many people prefer a morning shower, and that's fine, but a leisurely bath isn't just about cleanliness. It can be one of the fastest ways to cut ourselves off from the rest of the world and find a little calm after a long day. It shouldn't take you very long to fill up the tub or indulge in any other rituals you might want to include. Some people enjoy a good book and a glass of wine; others prefer bubbles, dim lights, and a few candles. You can even add some favorite music to the mix. There's no right or wrong to relax in the tub. Anyone who has already added a bath to their routine already knows how great it feels. Try one tonight and discover the benefits for yourself.

Boost Probiotics by Eating Active Culture Yogurt

Yogurt is an excellent source of calcium that also provides about 9 grams of animal protein per 6-ounce serving, plus vitamin B_2, vitamin B_{12}, potassium, and magnesium. One of the most beneficial aspects of yogurt comes from the use of active, good bacteria known as probiotics. To aid digestion, probiotics adjust the natural balance in the intestines of organisms known as microflora. To make sure your favorite brand of yogurt contains active cultures, look for labeling that says "live and active cultures," or for words such as *Bifidus regularis*, *L. bulgaricus*, *S. thermophilus*, or bifidobacterium. To make a tasty and healthy parfait that can help you incorporate yogurt into your diet, gather these ingredients:

* 2 tablespoons bran flakes cereal
* 4 ounces sugar-free vanilla yogurt
* ¼ cup sliced strawberries

Layer the ingredients in a tall cup, starting with the bran flakes, then the yogurt, and finally the strawberries.

Avoid Trans Fats

Artificial trans fat is produced when liquid vegetable oil is treated with heat, chemicals, and hydrogen to transform it into a product that is semisolid at room temperature. Even the process makes it sound very unhealthy, but food producers use it because it's inexpensive, performs well in both baked and deep-fried applications, keeps food fresher longer, and provides a nice "mouthfeel" to many products. Unfortunately, your body doesn't recognize these trans fats as an artificial substance, and so doesn't discard it in the digestion process. Instead, trans fat is fully incorporated into your cells, arteries, and veins, changing the functions and properties of your cells and of the enzymes that fuel your body. Sometimes knowing how something affects your body inspires you to eat healthier. Trans fat has been proven to affect our bodies negatively in many ways, including causing weight gain and increasing the risk of cancer. Foods high in trans fats include: margarine, fast food, baked goods, chips, crackers, cookies, and candy.

Plan Healthy Snacks
Ahead of Time

Eating daily snacks is a great way to make sure your metabolism is at its peak—as long as you're choosing healthy foods that provide important nutrients, and not a lot of fat or calories.

A healthy snack should be portion sensitive—a small amount of something nutritious—to keep the metabolic fires burning and tide you over to your next meal. Snacks should be small amounts of nutrient-dense foods ideally consisting of protein and carbohydrate. A few whole-wheat crackers with a wedge of farmer's cheese; a quarter-cup of cottage cheese with half an orange; a hard-boiled egg and half an apple; a slice of whole-wheat toast with thinly spread peanut butter. Plan your snacks just like you would your meals, so you make wise choices and have good foods available when you need them.

Make Your Own Sugar Body Scrub

Walk into any body-care shop and you'll find an array of salt and sugar scrubs that cost $20–$40 for one small jar. Exfoliating your skin doesn't have to be that expensive—and it's not just for women either. With a few simple ingredients you probably already have in your pantry, you can whip up a big batch of refreshing scrub. You will need:

* 1 cup brown sugar
* 1 cup white sugar
* Almond oil or vegetable oil
* Essential oil or fragrance oil (try lemon, vanilla, lavender, or rose)

Mix both the brown and white sugars in a medium-sized mixing bowl. Add the almond or vegetable oil to the sugar until it becomes a thick paste. Add a few drops of your favorite essential or fragrance oil. Make sure you aren't allergic to any of the oils you want to use.

Jump in the shower and rub the mixture all over your body, paying close attention to typically dry areas like elbows and feet.

Get a Biofeedback Analysis

Biofeedback is a technique some people use to gain awareness of how their bodies function in an effort to reduce stress. A practitioner will connect a client to a machine to explore involuntary body functions, such as blood pressure and heart rate. The machine may beep or flash when the client tenses, encouraging her to do something different. You can learn how certain actions, such as laughing, talking softly, and even positive thoughts, positively impact bodily functions. After seeing proof of how these behaviors calm down your body, you can make conscious choices to work them into your everyday life. Enthusiasts insist that, over time, biofeedback also retrains the automatic nervous system to be healthier.

Take Care of Your Eyesight with a Super Juice

Carotene is especially helpful for your eyes, but also helps the liver. In addition to providing a great energy boost, it's also believed to aid in preventing the onset of Type 2 diabetes. To make this Super Carotene Combo Juice, gather these ingredients:

* 3 medium carrots, trimmed
* ½ large cantaloupe, peeled and seeded
* 1 medium sweet potato, peeled and cut into chunks
* 1 tablespoon fresh mint leaves

1. Process the carrots through an electronic juicer according to the manufacturer's directions.
2. Cut the cantaloupe into chunks and add. Add the sweet potato.
3. Roll the mint leaves into a ball to compress and add to the juicer.
4. Whisk the juice together and serve over ice, if desired. Garnish with additional mint leaves for extra eye appeal. Yields 1½ cups.

Boost Your Self-Esteem
with Orgasms

Even before the scientists step in, it's easy to believe that having orgasms can make you feel good about yourself. Orgasms are intensely pleasurable, and you can't help but be impressed that your body is able to produce such sensations. If you're giving yourself an orgasm, your confidence should feel that much higher. Beyond that, science shows that having orgasms can actually improve your self-esteem because of the chemicals they release. During orgasm, blood flows into the prefrontal cortex of the right side of the brain. This part of your brain is responsible for decision making and personality expression, and when stimulated by the orgasm, it makes the body feel a profound sense of gratification.

Gratitude isn't the only benefit of orgasm, though. Orgasms also can reduce the effects of depression, because they release endorphins, hormones that improve mood. So the next time you've got the body image blues or your self-esteem is in a slump, don't reach for the jelly doughnuts or sit there feeling sad. Try having an orgasm—either on your own or with someone you love—and lift your spirits the natural way!

Try Out Adaptogens

American ginseng, eleuthero, rhodiola, and holy basil are just a few examples of the plants that we now know as adaptogens. These remarkable plants have been shown to have a gentle but measurable influence on immunity, sleep, stress levels, energy, and endurance. Many of these were first used many generations ago in Ayurveda (the traditional system of herbalism in India) and in traditional Chinese medicine (TCM). Adaptogens can become a valuable part of your self-care routine. Thanks to their safety (an herb must be nontoxic and safe for extended use to qualify as an adaptogen), they are some of the easiest and most accessible herbs to work with for the everyday person.

Make Your Own Facial Cream
with Essential Oils

Facial creams are emulsions, or mixtures of oil and water. They also might contain essential oils, which impart a scent and treat specific skin conditions. Use one of the following, based on your skin type:

* Lavender for all skin types
* Chamomile for sensitive skin
* Grapefruit for oily skin
* Rose, also known as damask rose, rose otto, or Bulgarian rose, for all skin types, especially dry and/or sensitive

Here's a cream you can make at home:

* ⅔ cup distilled water
* ⅓ cup aloe vera gel
* 1 or 2 drops of essential oil (see options)
* ¾ cup apricot oil
* ⅓ cup coconut oil or cocoa butter
* ¼ teaspoon lanolin
* ½ to 1 ounce beeswax, grated

1. Combine the distilled water, aloe gel, and essential oil in a glass cup or bowl, and set aside.
2. In a double boiler over low heat, combine the apricot oil, coconut oil (or cocoa butter), lanolin, and beeswax, and heat them just enough to melt the beeswax. Remove from heat.
3. Pour the oil mixture into a blender and allow it to cool completely. When it's room temperature, turn the blender on to its highest speed and add the water mixture, pouring as slowly as you can, to the oils. Don't pour the whole amount at once—watch the mixture closely, and when it looks thick and white, stop adding water. Pour the cream into glass jars. Store in a cool location.

Don't Ignore Pain

Everyone feels pain periodically, especially while exercising. Only the easiest of workouts will be pain-free. The stress of pushing your muscles and tendons to another level, which is how you gain in strength and endurance, will bring some discomfort. For example, if you are doing some hill training, running, or biking, it's going to hurt as you push yourself up that incline. If your swim session is focused on increasing your speed, your shoulders will be burning as you get to the end of the pool each time.

All that is normal. It is an entirely different matter when you experience unexpected or sharp pain, whether exercising or not. When that happens, the alarm bells should start going off. It is a mistake with potentially serious consequences to ignore acute pain. Whatever you are doing, if you feel a sharp pain, stop your activity. Give yourself a few minutes, then resume whatever you were doing. If the pain persists, it's time to figure out what's wrong. Find a healthcare professional who can diagnose your problem and prescribe the most effective treatments.

Give Yourself a Foot Massage Using Reflexology

A foot massage can feel like heaven, but did you know that it can benefit other parts of the body as well? Reflexology is the practice of massaging specific areas of the feet in order to affect other parts of your body. Much like acupuncture and Reiki, reflexology works by changing the flow of a person's chi, or life-force energy, to promote healing. Different areas of the foot correspond with different body systems. For example, the tops of your toes correspond with your brain, the inner arch of the foot matches the stomach, and the lower foot and heel match the colon and bladder. Look online for a map of the foot and the body parts affected when you massage them. You can give yourself a massage or give one to your partner.

Try a Sauna or Steam Bath

Taking a sauna or steam bath can eliminate toxins and excess sodium, improve circulation, loosen tense and sore muscles, and enable you to relax into your happy place. (Always make sure that you are in good health by checking with your physician before stepping into a sauna or steam room.) To make the most of your sauna experience, savor the feeling you get when you open the door to leave the room. The rush of cool air hitting your skin after spending time in a steam bath or sauna is one of the best natural highs there is. It is an energizing and exhilarating way to end a relaxing activity. With a clear head and a relaxed body, life might not seem so difficult after all. Be sure to drink lots of water when you're done to replace what you lose from perspiration!

Maintain Your Ability to Balance

It has happened to us all at some point—tripping over a parking block or missing that last step. As you age, the process of balancing that is controlled by the nervous system begins to slow down. This slowing down process is inevitable, but with training you can maintain your agility. Believe it or not, human beings lose most of their natural balance after only age twenty-five! Practicing balance exercises challenges the nervous system and helps keep the mind-body connection sharp as well. Ask your doctor or personal trainer which balance exercises, such as yoga or Pilates, might be right for you.

Exercise Your Brain Too!

Numerous studies have shown that people who lead lives with little mental stimulation experience greater cognitive loss as they age. Their memory fails with greater frequency, and they find it increasingly difficult to work puzzles, perform mathematic equations, and do other mental feats that come quite easily to people who "exercise" their brains often. Maintaining mental acuity is like training to be a professional athlete; you need to do something every day that revs up your brain and flexes your gray matter. Treat your brain like a muscle, one that needs a strenuous workout on a regular basis. Do crossword or number puzzles for fun brain challenges.

Eat More Lean Protein

Proteins, which are made up of amino acids, work within the body as primary building blocks for all tissues and cells, including your muscles. Their secondary function is to provide energy after your carbohydrate resources have been depleted—thereby boosting your metabolism. One gram of protein equals 4 calories and it can be found in meat, fish, eggs, dairy, and legumes (beans and peas).

A study published in the *American Journal of Clinical Nutrition* found that when people ate more protein and cut down on fat, they reduced their calorie intake by 441 calories a day. In fact, experts think that eating protein actually enhances the effect of leptin, a hormone that helps the body feel full. When you choose protein, reach for the healthier choices, such as fish, skinless chicken, lean pork, tofu, nuts, beans, eggs, and low-fat dairy products, with the occasional lean red meat.

Invite a Friend to Help You Get Healthier

If you've decided to live a healthier lifestyle, maybe it's time to get your friends involved. Go shopping together for the ingredients to make a healthy, homemade meal. Enlist one or more friends to help you discover interesting ways to prepare heart-healthy entrées. Split the cost of a cookbook for healthy meals or find some recipes online and, with your friends, cook something a little spicy, saucy, or just sensational, certain to delight your senses. Plan an informal dinner party after you go for a long walk or take an exercise class together.

Have a Cup of Chamomile Tea

Chamomile tea is widely known for its relaxing properties as well as its apple-like aroma, and is known to soothe the nerves and restore vitality. Contemporary herbalists also recommend chamomile for fever, digestive upsets, anxiety, and insomnia. British researchers recently discovered that chamomile stimulates the immune system's white blood cells. It's particularly recommended for use at the onset of a cold or the flu and its warming and soothing properties promote sleep, the greatest curative of all. Drink a cup or two of tea for relaxation, or at night to promote sleep. Caution: generally speaking, chamomile is one of the safest herbs available. However, if you are allergic to ragweed or have ever suffered anaphylactic shock, avoid this herb.

Go Slow and Steady When Lifting Weights

People who are new to weight training often use the momentum that results from swinging weights to do the movements. But you instead want to move with intentional control. Weight training is one of those activities where you need to pay attention so you force yourself to keep it challenging. The specific number of pounds that you lift is not important; you get stronger over time. What's important is that you are able to execute your exercises in a slow and controlled manner with good posture. This is how you will improve your strength.

When you use your muscles and not momentum, you should be able to lower the weight and lift it with control. Since many movements are assisted by gravity on the way down, slow movements challenge your muscles. If you simply drop weights on the way down, you risk hurting yourself or damaging equipment—and it's painful on the eardrums. Fast, jerky movements mean you're not maximizing your training benefits. Instead, execute your exercises smoothly through a full range of motion.

Readjust Your Portion Control Meter

Ever since we entered the supersize era, Americans have grown much heavier—and our ability to judge what constitutes a healthy portion of food has been skewed. To follow a healthy diet, you may need to readjust your visual image of desirable portions in each food group. Portion sizes are meant as general guidelines and vary according to your sex and age, so ask your doctor what's right for you. Use these visual comparisons to help estimate your portion sizes:

* A 3-ounce portion of cooked meat, poultry, or fish is about the size of a deck of playing cards.
* A medium potato is about the size of a computer mouse.
* A cup of rice or pasta is about the size of a fist or a tennis ball.
* A teaspoon of peanut butter equals one die; 2 tablespoons is about the size of a golf ball.
* An ounce of snack foods—pretzels, etc.—equals a large handful.

Practice Aromatherapy
with Essential Oils

Aromatherapy is the practice of using aromatic plants to treat various conditions and maintain well-being. Modern aromatherapy uses essential oils, which are volatile liquids distilled in a way that selects miniscule molecules and leaves behind heavier plant waxes, oils, and other materials. Aromatherapy is practiced by aerial diffusion, direct inhalation, and topical application (via massage). Experts theorize that it works in two ways. The first is through aroma, which moves through the olfactory system to stimulate limbic (emotional) centers of the brain. The other is through a direct pharmacological effect: the oils' beneficial compounds are delivered via the skin or mucous membranes. Popular medicinal herbs used in aromatherapy include:

* Lavender is used for anxiety, insomnia, mild depression, and hair loss (alopecia).
* Chamomile treats insomnia, anxiety, indigestion, skin infections, wounds, and inflammation.
* Eucalyptus is a decongestant, expectorant, and headache remedy.
* Peppermint relieves indigestion, coughs, nausea, and headaches.

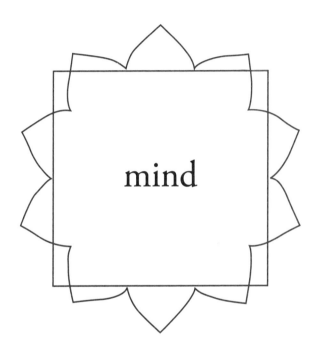

mind

Design a Goal Board

We all have a lot of goals and aspirations in life, but seeing them every day reminds us to continue to reach for them in our everyday tasks. Use a corkboard or dry-erase board and draw or cut out pictures or phrases that represent the ultimate job you want or that dream home you have been saving for. Make sure to hang this board in your home where you will see it every morning before you start your day. Whatever the goal may be, the visual daily reminder will help you focus your energy and get your creative juices flowing every time you see the board.

Learn a Different Language

Most of us wish we had paid more attention in our required language classes in high school. Not only is it helpful when traveling, but on your resume it can add tremendous value when you can speak more than one language. Studies show that only 5.5 percent of the world speaks English as a primary language. You can take classes online, purchase a book, or take classes at your local college. Learning a new language will not only increase your global understanding, but it will also open up new opportunities for you. There are more than 6,500 different languages spoken in the world today, so pick one and start studying. Expand your mind!

Create a Budget

Self-care should be comprehensive—and that means caring for your financial future as well as your body, mind, and spirit. It may seem tedious at first, but making a budget is truly rewarding in the long run. Putting your expenses in writing can help you plan for that future vacation or help you pay off that burdensome college debt. Whatever the reason may be, sit down with a pen and paper or at the computer and organize your monthly income and expenditures to take a closer look at where your money is going. Seeing your money in a more organized way can help you plan for the future and avoid those unsettling "money crunch" moments.

Choose Your News

With all the negative messages coming at you every day from myriad directions, you may wonder how you can possibly feel optimistic about anything. One strategy to combat this problem is to be more selective about the news items you read. If you'd like a change from your current source, look at websites like www.world-newspapers.com for lists of magazines and newspapers from all over the world. Another way to avoid all of the negativity and to maintain a more positive, balanced emotional state is to take a break from the news for two days. Then evaluate just how much of an impact the news has been having on your sense of well-being. The answer may surprise you. After that, you may need to more closely examine your relationship with these media outlets. By taking that break, you will have the insight and tools necessary to be able to do this.

Identify Precisely What Is Causing Your Stress

Often, when you feel "stressed out," it is a generalized feeling of stress. If you take a moment to examine your situation, however, you will find that your feelings are actually the cumulative result of numerous individual pressures that have finally reached the boiling point. One of the first steps toward learning how to manage stress is to identify these individual pressures. The next time you start to feel overwhelmed and stressed out, ask yourself the following questions to determine what is causing these emotions:

* Am I overcommitted?
* Am I taking care of others and neglecting my own self-care?
* Am I trying to accomplish everything on my own without asking for any support from anyone else?
* What is going on in my life right now that gives me a sense of struggle?
* Is what I stress over more important than my health and happiness?

It's always worth learning how to manage your stress— all of the tips in this book will help you do just that.

Take a Mental Vacation

For instant relaxation, try imagery and visualization. Feeling stressed? Feeling anxious? Feeling hopeless? Go on vacation. No, don't leave your desk and head to the airport. Stay at your desk, close your eyes, relax, breathe, and use your imagination to visualize the place you would most like to be.

You remember your imagination, don't you? It was that thing that, as a child, allowed you to fly like a bird, stomp like an elephant, bark like a dog, save the world from disaster, go on safari, jump from an airplane with your parachute, and visit a land made entirely out of candy, all in one day. Wasn't that fun? Your imagination is still in your head, even if it's grown a little rusty from disuse. Time to take it out, brush it off, and use it in the service of self-care! Let yourself daydream a little. Consider it personal time to recharge. It's fun, and it's also an excellent way to manage the stress that comes your way. After all, that's what vacations are for!

Learn to Meditate

In the late 1960s, Harvard cardiologist Herbert Benson, MD, discovered that relaxation methods counterbalanced the body's response to "fight or flight." He called this the "relaxation response." Benson's tests showed that people who meditate—meaning simply sitting quietly with their minds focused on a single word, idea, or thought—could slow their heart and respiratory rates and encourage relaxation.

The brain is a complex and amazing organ, and meditation can teach you to harness your mind's power, integrate your mind and body, and feed your hungry spirit. Meditation comes in many forms, including sitting meditation, walking meditation, mindfulness meditation, yoga meditation, mantra meditation, mandala meditation, visualization, and even prayer.

Solve Sex Stress

Sexual imbalances can create stress on a relationship. These occur when one partner wants more sex than the other, or a different type of sex. Each relationship is unique, and there is no set formula to solve all your problems in the bedroom. Brainstorm ideas to decrease sex stress—scheduling two nights a week, using direct commands during lovemaking, getting a toy—to solve the challenges you face, and put them into practice. Experiment with different ideas until you've minimized the sources of stress. The health of your sexual life is a direct reflection of the health of your relationship, so keeping life hot is key to relationship bliss.

Don't Give In to Gossip

Friends need to keep the trust they have placed in each other, and you want to uphold your end of the friendship bargain by being trustworthy. We live and work in worlds (in person and online) populated by friends, acquaintances, family members, and coworkers, and those people often are separated only by degrees. It really is a small world. Although a friend or relative might want to know all the latest gossip, don't share other people's problems. That's no one else's business. Your friends will rest easier knowing they can share personal issues with you, and you'll feel better knowing you're a thoughtful, caring friend.

Get a Low-Maintenance Pet

Doctors have aquariums in their waiting rooms to calm and entertain their waiting patients. Studies have shown that watching fish in an aquarium can actually lower your blood pressure. There is some cost involved, but if you're willing to spend a little money and to invest some time in research and maintenance, an aquarium can be a wonderful way to enjoy your free time.

Visit a nearby pet store to check out the tropical fish. Knowledgeable staff can help you select the aquarium and fish perfect for you—and your budget. After you get the right tank and the right fish, you'll have a lot to enjoy. You'll have a pastime that includes living creatures and their environment, the chance to learn more about a very popular hobby, and something that's going to look nice wherever you put it. Most hobbies don't reward you with that many benefits. And remember, you won't have to take your pet fish for a walk three times a day!

Chill Out If You Can't Sleep

Don't get all stressed out about not being able to get to sleep. An occasional night of too-few ZZZs won't hurt you as long as you *usually* get enough sleep. Rather than lying in the dark, tossing and turning in frustration, turn on the light and find something to read. Get comfortable. Sip some warm milk or chamomile tea. Meditate. Steer your mind away from worries and think about pleasant things— not sleep, just pleasant things. Breathe. Even if you don't get to sleep, at least you'll get to relax. And you'll probably feel drowsy soon.

However, if it becomes a pattern that keeps happening, figure out why. Maybe you've been working right up to the time you crawl beneath the sheets, not giving your mind enough time to transition from stress to rest. Perhaps you've been watching the news or a television show that riled up feelings. Once you identify what could be contributing, talk to your doctor about it.

Put Together a Puzzle

Putting together a jigsaw puzzle can be challenging but fun, depending on the pattern and number of pieces. Go out and buy one with a design you really like. This could be an all-day project, so it is best saved for a rainy day or if you are snowed in. When you are finished, you can glue all of the pieces together and put it in a frame. The great thing about puzzles is that they come in a variety of challenge levels. You can do a 100-piece puzzle or a 1,000-piece puzzle, depending on how much time you have. If you really want a challenge, pick up a 3-D puzzle. You can have your very own model of the White House, the Empire State Building, or the *Millennium Falcon*.

Break the Cycle of
Bad Relationships

Do you continually fall for people who are wrong for you? You're not alone, but it's time to break the cycle. For example, if you crave excitement, instead of winding up in a relationship drama all the time, try finding someone who loves to travel to exotic locations or who participates in high-adrenaline sports. By finding other, healthier ways to fulfill what you need, you're more likely to have a long-lasting and fulfilling relationship with less drama.

You can also look back at previous relationships to try to find some patterns. You're going to need a quiet space and some time to take an unflinchingly honest look at your past relationships. (If you'd like moral support or some candid input, enlist the help of a trusted friend.) For each past romance, list why you were attracted to that person in the first place, and then write down why the relationship didn't work out. See if you can identify any similarities, then brainstorm ways to get what you want in a healthy relationship.

Unwind When You Get Home

You may have a variety of ways to unwind at the end of a busy workday. For example, you may like to have a cup of tea or listen to some music. Whatever is it, it's important for you to have a ritual conducive to unwinding. Let it be something you look forward to, but that does not create an additional stress in your life (from trying to pay for it, keep it clean, etc.). Keep it simple but pleasurable. The transition from a high-stress workday to your home life needs carved-out time (and space, if possible).

Color

As a kid, you probably spent hours coloring with markers, crayons, and colored pencils. You would try to be very careful to stay inside the lines. Coloring can still be a fun and relaxing activity. Go out and buy your favorite coloring tool, whether it's a sixty-four pack of crayons, thin markers, or colored pencils. Pick up a coloring book as well. Spend the afternoon coloring away. You won't have to worry about staying inside the lines now, so that should take the pressure off.

Visit a Different Country

Make it a goal to visit a different country this year. Whether you choose a neighboring country close to home or one overseas, experiencing another culture is truly an eye-opening experience. Remember that a vacation is not always relaxing, and you should map out times for rest and for exploring. When preparing for your trip, do research on the country's currency, language, and customs. Try to familiarize yourself with their laws and regulations to stay out of trouble. Always know where your nearest US embassy is located in case of an emergency. Finally, make sure you have a large and empty memory card for all those memorable snapshots.

Be Positive

Optimistic thinking focuses on what's going well in life—the beautiful, the fun, and the well-done rather than the ugly, boring, and potentially hazardous. An optimist sees a glass half full, as the saying goes, and even puts a flower in it. Why? Seeing life as beautiful and fun increases not only your own happiness but also the happiness of those around you. Whenever you are faced with a tough situation, do your best to see all of it—including potential silver linings. Staying positive helps you weather life's storms, big and small.

Create a Family Mission Statement

Family life can be fulfilling and wonderful, but it can also bring some stress into your life. To bring your family together with a common goal and give everyone a feeling of purpose and belonging, all you'll need is a pen and some paper. If you have a dry-erase board and some markers, that's even better. Gather everyone in the family together and explain that you're going to create a mission statement—a written declaration that expresses the intentions, purpose, and priorities of the family.

1. Ask each person to suggest words to describe your family. What kind of behavior is acceptable and unacceptable? What are your family's goals? Put some of the ideas in sentence form. For example, "The Turner family treats each other with respect, and they respect the privacy of everyone in the family."

2. Write down as many sentences as you need to convey the thoughts represented in the brainstorming session. Revise the words down to the bare minimum.

3. Print out the mission statement, have everyone sign and date it, and post it in a prominent place where it won't be forgotten. Don't forget to revise it as needed.

Write a Novel

November marks National Novel Writing Month, or NaNoWriMo (www.nanowrimo.org)—a project for aspiring writers, veterans of the craft, or anyone who wants to give writing a try. The premise is to write a 50,000-word novel in one month. It sounds like a huge amount of pressure to be creative, but if you go to the website, you'll realize that it's a pretty casual affair. Nobody's going to twist your arm to write that novel. Pride and money are not on the line. The idea behind the site is to celebrate the wonderful world of writing and to engage your creative side. It's an exercise that exists for the joy of craft.

You don't have to wait until November to play around with the idea of a novel, though. You don't even have to write a novel. Simply take an hour or two every night or every other night to sit down at your desk or at your laptop and write. Don't think about it. Don't let your brain swell with visions of glory or the stress of coming up with something everyone is going to like. Let go of those notions and get lost in the pleasure of writing something. It can be a poem, a short story, a screenplay, a novel, or anything that gets the keys clicking.

Save Money with a Vacation Jar

You'd like your next getaway to be terrific, but you're worried about money. Saving for anything is a pretty abstract goal, but here's a way to make it concrete. You'll need a large jar or another item suitable for collecting money. You can purchase large, decorative jars online or just recycle a clean food container. (To take it a step further, collect some pictures from magazines or travel brochures of places you want to visit and decorate your jar!) Place the container in a conspicuous place, and make sure that all the money saved for the vacation goes into the jar. This is an especially powerful exercise in an age when most people don't use cash very often! Make a point of periodically counting how much money has accumulated. It's a well-known fact that there's a connection between how much effort and sacrifice goes into something and how much we appreciate it.

Put Photos in Albums

Do you have boxes of photo prints stored in a closet, or hundreds of digital photos on your hard drive? Get them into an album as soon as possible. Not only does this organize them, but it also helps protect them from getting ruined or lost. Whether you make albums on a computer or by hand, you'll be so glad that you did. The computer is a great place to store these memories, but having them in a tangible form makes it easier to enjoy those people and places on a regular basis.

Calm Anxiety with Herbs

Anxiety disorders share a common feature: an uncontrollable and, in many cases unexplainable, fear or dread. In most cases, people with one type of anxiety disorder have another; anxiety disorders frequently accompany depression, as well. While serious anxiety disorders demand attention from a doctor (and may require the use of prescription drugs), many milder or episodic types of anxiety respond well to herbal remedies. For example:

* **HOPS:** This is a traditional treatment that helps relieve depression, as well. Hops also acts as a mild sedative.
* **KAVA:** Kava is the go-to herbal for anxiety, and has centuries of use (and research) behind it. The latest studies confirm its ability to relieve the symptoms of anxiety as well as the most frequently prescribed pharmaceuticals.
* **PASSIONFLOWER:** Research has shown that passionflower relieves anxiety symptoms as well as drugs, without the side effects. Other research shows it can relieve presurgery anxiety without unnecessary sedation.
* **VALERIAN:** Valerian is a gentle sedative and mood stabilizer. Research shows that combining it with Saint John's wort or kava can relieve agitation and anxiety.

Enjoy a Day of Silence

Set a date when you have nothing planned to enjoy a day of complete silence. Let your family and loved ones know that you will not be picking up the phone or answering any emails. This will cut down on the worried voicemails and texts that you will receive. If needed, create a password for others, like three phone calls in a row, that could signal an emergency. This day should not include television, music, or any other "noisy" distractions. Silence can help us do some soul searching or simply allow us to pay attention to the amount of vocalizing we do every day. Curl up on the couch with a good book or magazine and let those vocal cords take a nice rest.

Celebrate with Bubbly

Even if you don't have a special occasion like an anniversary or birthday to celebrate, break out a good bottle of bubbly (nonalcoholic works just as well) and a fancy champagne flute. To make it even more special, put a strawberry in the drink. You can do this by yourself or with a loved one. Give a toast to honor something you are proud of or happy about today. A little sense of occasion on an otherwise boring night will make you feel special. Don't forget that just waking up in the morning is a reason to celebrate.

Network

Some people falsely believe that you don't need to begin to network until you are looking for a job. That would be akin to starting to take better care of your body after you have been diagnosed with heart disease. It's a much better idea to try to stay healthy in the first place with regular exercise and a balanced diet. Think of networking the same way; it's something you can do to keep your career healthy.

Building a network can seem like an overwhelming task, especially if you think you are starting without any contacts at all. Well, guess what? You already have contacts—relatives, friends, and acquaintances. Sure, not all of them can personally help you with your career—they probably don't even work in the same field you do—but they have friends and acquaintances who may be able to help. Members of your network can offer you advice on work-related matters, provide information, hook you up with potential clients, and even help you find a job. The larger your network, the more opportunities you'll find to get help achieving your goals.

Plan a Stress-Free Vacation

Are you looking forward to your next vacation? Even if your family doesn't include children, you still have the stress of dealing with your spouse and other family members. A poorly planned family vacation can be very stressful, and that's not what you want in a vacation. Take a look at your vacation plans and see if you can reduce or eliminate potential stressors. Given the purpose of a family vacation—creating memories and fun as a family—it's important to manage as many of the possible problems as you can, so that your family vacation can be everything you hope for and more. Here are some potential problems to try to avoid:

* Adults hit a vacation burned out or tired already.
* Sitting in a car, train, or other source of transportation for longer than normal.
* Eating out and trying new cuisine upsets the body's usual dietary habits and digestion.
* Not planning outings and making restaurant reservations ahead of time.
* Family members have different expectations and conflict arises when everyone's expectations are not met.

Keep a Journal for a Year

Time goes by so fast that we often forget to stop and recognize what we've accomplished or taken part in throughout the year. Starting today, keep a journal and write in it every day for a year. At the end of the year, you'll be amazed at what you did, how you felt, and what you got through. This is a great way to reflect on the past and also make plans for the future. You'll learn from your mistakes as well as remember the great times you had. In ten years, you can pull out that journal and have a laugh. You'll likely find that what you thought was important wasn't, and you'll see how much you've changed.

Make a New Year's Resolution

Make a resolution this year and stick to it. It may be helpful to create your resolution list a few weeks before the first of the year to help you prepare. If committing to a few things is too stressful, focus all your energy on one important goal. If you plan to quit smoking or start a new exercise schedule, spend the few weeks leading up to New Year's doing your research and creating a realistic strategy to help you succeed. Create a timeline of the weeks and months after New Year's where you schedule rewards to help motivate yourself to stay focused. Make this year the best one it can be!

Control Demanding Schedules

Demanding schedules involving work, children, and community obligations can make it difficult to administer any self-care. Regaining control means giving up something to create blocks of time to be with yourself and the people important to you. Here are some ways to fit time with loved ones into your busy life:

1. Communicate often, sharing your feelings of love.
2. Establish small rituals, such as sharing breakfast, an evening walk, or kisses before bed.
3. Do volunteer activities together when possible.
4. Eliminate time wasters such as watching television.
5. Make a master schedule of a month of activities for the whole family and pencil in appointments for family time. Also, make time to talk about how you can get a better handle on your schedules in the future.

Learn How to Play
a Musical Instrument

It is never too late to learn how to play an instrument. Choose something that will work for you in your daily life. If you can't afford to buy a piano but want to learn how to play, an inexpensive keyboard is a great choice. If you are someone who would like to take your instrument with you, try learning how to play the guitar or violin. It doesn't matter what instrument you choose; any of them will help expand your mind and focus your energy on something other than your stress. If you can't afford to take proper lessons, try one of the many tutorials online where you can teach yourself.

Turn Off the Television

On average, Americans watch over five hours of television a day. Do yourself a favor and turn off the tube for twenty-four hours. If you're worried you'll be bored to tears, make a list of all the things you can do when you're not wasting time watching television. Do a little home decorating or try a new recipe you've never made before. Start reading a new novel or write one of your own. Invite some friends over for a night of fun. Nothing on television is better than spending time with loved ones.

Divide Up Chores

According to a recent survey by the Pew Research Center, sharing the household chores is a very important factor in a successful relationship. Some couples decide that the person who makes the dinner does not have to clean up; the other person will take care of it. Many couples also designate a certain day to do the general housecleaning and other chores. Children, from toddlers to teens, can and should help with household chores as well. The point is to get everyone to pitch in to help keep the family home and pets clean and cared for.

To avoid squabbles about whose turn it is to do which chores, make a family chore chart. You can make your own, or simply search the Internet and find chore charts and lists already compiled and ready to download. You can then personalize them with photos, affirmations, or quotations.

Know the Warning Signs
of a Workaholic

You love your job. You work hard . . . okay, maybe *too* hard. One of the many signs of being a workaholic is working more than forty hours a week. However, it is possible that you simply have a strong work ethic and are not a workaholic. The difference is that the workaholic cannot live a life in balance by prioritizing activities and leaving work at work. In addition:

1. They think about work when they should be focusing on driving or changing the baby.
2. They believe working long hours is justified if they love the work.
3. They hate being interrupted by family and others who want them to do something else.
4. They permit relationships to suffer because of work.
5. They often worry about being laid off or fired even when their present job is secure.

Pull your life back into balance by modifying your schedule so as not to devote a lot of time to things that are not a priority. Seek professional counseling if old patterns of allowing work to fill all your time begin to re-emerge.

Get Through the Breakup Blues

When you're trying to find ways to get through a lonely night after a breakup, *never* just lie in bed in the dark and contemplate your situation. Here are some quick-fix ideas to get you through:

* Write down your feelings in a dating journal. You'll find that the process is habit-forming, especially when you are feeling down.
* Wash your hair. It's a cleansing experience, literally and figuratively. Tubs are another relaxing option. Light some candles. Sit, soak, relax! Replace sad thoughts with thoughts of things you love.
* Work it out. If you've got equipment or tapes at home, get moving, no matter how late it is. Exercise produces a chemical reaction in your body that elevates your mood. Or just dance to whatever music moves you.

Spend the Day with Your Pet

Studies have shown that owning a pet can reduce stress and provide excellent health benefits. If you spend just a few minutes petting your dog or cat, your mood improves, blood pressure goes down, and breathing becomes more relaxed. Having a pet that needs to be walked means you are getting exercise as well. If you have a dog, check out your local dog park, where both you and your pet can make new friends. Today, spend the whole day with your pet. If you don't have one, ask a friend if you can take her dog for a walk or relax with her cat. Or consider adopting one from your local animal shelter.

Write Your Memoir

We all have a story to tell, and one of the most cathartic things you can do is get it out. Make an outline that highlights all of the major events of your life. Think of the most important thing that has happened to you and focus your story on that. Everyone is unique and everyone is interesting in their own way. Find out what has made your life different and what has made you who you are. This memoir can be just for you; you don't have to show it to anyone else if you don't want to. If you are very ambitious, try writing your family's history. Reflecting on your past will make you appreciate what's to come.

Be on Time and Be Prepared!

If you want to get on the wrong side of your family, friends, and coworkers, make a habit of showing up late and unprepared for events. If you need some help making it to events on time, try these two simple but effective ideas:

1. Set an alarm on your smartphone. Add your appointments, then add reminders using the alarm or ring tone.
2. Make a point of giving yourself some extra time to get where you need to be. This will allow some cushion if anything unexpectedly goes awry.

Build a Playlist of Relaxing Music

If you can't seem to relax, create a mix of music that will transition you into a peaceful mood. Choose songs that calm you down. Be mindful not to include those slow melodies that remind you of sad memories. Organize the songs from the fastest tempo to the slowest, and consider starting with tunes with lyrics and ending with classical. This natural progression will assist you in slowing down. Make yourself a cup of tea, sit back, and enjoy the serene melodies.

Change One Thing You Don't Like about Yourself

We all have one thing we don't like about ourselves. Maybe you worry too much or are afraid to take a risk. Maybe you want to eat healthier or want to commit to incorporating exercise into your daily routine. Today, make the commitment to change—there's no better time than the present. If you are thinking, "It's too late; I'm too old to change," think again; it's never too late to improve yourself. It won't be easy at first, so take it one step at a time. Just saying, "Yes, I'm ready to change that part of my life," is a huge step.

Take a Class for Fun at a Local College

If you've always wanted to take a creative writing course or a class on western civilization, sign up today at your local college. If you haven't been to school in a long time, don't be nervous; you'll find many students like you who just want to learn something new. Since this is for fun, it takes the pressure off when it comes to tests and finals. Learning shouldn't stop just because you are no longer in school. Get a list of courses offered and pick one that sounds interesting.

Make a Family Tree

Discovering where you came from can give you great insight into who you are now. Trace your roots back to their beginnings by making a family tree. Ask relatives if they can help fill in the blanks or go online to try and find public records that might give you clues about family members who have passed away. There are many websites that can help you trace your ancestry, like www.ancestry.com. You can create your family tree and search for other relatives on the website.

Choose a Mentor

Whether you work for yourself or for a large corporation, choosing a mentor is something you should consider. A mentor can be a valuable source of wisdom and experience and provide you with opportunities to network with other individuals in your field. Pick someone you respect and ask her to mentor you. Most people will be pleased and flattered to pass along advice or act as a sounding board for ideas you have. Here is how to approach such a relationship:

1. When you meet with your new mentor for the first time, introduce yourself and explain why you're looking for a mentor. Thank him or her for the help.
2. Make sure that both of you agree to and understand the limits in terms of time, contact, and extent of personal involvement.
3. Create a schedule for regular meetings.
4. If it makes either of you more comfortable, you might want to put these details in writing.

Curb Worrywart Tendencies

Are you a worrywart? How many of the following describe you?

* You find yourself worrying about things that are extremely unlikely, such as suffering from a freak accident or developing an illness you have no reason to believe you would develop.
* You often lose sleep worrying about what would happen to you if you lost a loved one, or what would happen to your loved ones if they lost you.
* You feel compelled to control the behaviors of others because you worry that they can't take care of themselves.
* You are overly cautious about engaging in any behavior that could result in harm or hurt to you or to those around you, even if the risk is small (such as driving a car, flying in an airplane, or visiting a big city).

If even a couple of these worrywart characteristics describes you, you probably worry more than you have to. Make a list of ten things you can do to reduce your stress. Also, list all those worries and then assess the real possibility that each will come to pass. Often we worry needlessly, and life is just too short!

Go on a Staycation

A staycation is the same as a vacation, but you stay at home. You don't fly off to a Caribbean island or go on an expensive, lavish holiday. During troubling economic times, a staycation is the best way to save a few bucks while enjoying some much-needed time off. Think of all the things you can do while at home or close to home: you can decorate that second bedroom, visit the park or zoo, bake cookies, have friends over for a party, swim at the beach, or spend time with your family. The importance of a vacation is to have some down time and recharge your batteries. What better location to accomplish both of those than home? You won't have to worry about lost luggage, missed flights, bad room service, or tourist traps. Plan your staycation today!

Take a Mental Health Day

With all of the stress that follows us from day to day, sometimes you just need to recuperate and rebalance yourself. A mental health day does just that. Take the day off from work today and decompress: go shopping, eat out for lunch, do yoga, get a massage. Erase responsibility and stress from your life for twenty-four hours. You'll come back to work refreshed and ready to take on anything.

Learn to Delegate

When you're working on a large project, do you try to take everything on all by yourself or do you try to divide the tasks among your coworkers? If you're the type to put in long hours to complete a project that would be better served by multiple brains and hands, it's time to learn how to delegate as part of a self-care routine. Break down the project into smaller parts. Are there parts you're overseeing that another colleague is more qualified to deal with? If it's all right with your manager, assign it to that person. Then be ready to collect their portions of the project and integrate them into the whole.

Practice Mindfulness

Being mindful simply means being aware of the present. Don't just smile at your spouse—notice the color of his eyes, his hair, the way his chin curves, the hair sticking out of his ears. Don't just eat your sandwich—notice the slippery meat, the salty pickle, the crunchy lettuce against your tongue. Vietnamese Buddhist monk and meditation guru Thich Nhat Hanh teaches that mindfulness is enjoying life now. Hanh encourages beginners to start with an orange, a particularly juicy and sweet fruit. Smell the orange as you open it. Feel the peel against your hand. Savor the exploding juice inside your mouth as you take a bite. Think of nothing in the world but that orange. This, Hanh teaches, is peace.

Cope with Shyness

If you consider yourself shy, you aren't alone. According to a study published by Lynne Henderson and Philip Zimbardo in the *Encyclopedia of Mental Health*, approximately 50 percent of people surveyed considered themselves to be shy. Shyness can impact your life in many ways. While you may be able to interact with people with whom you are familiar, talking to strangers can be very difficult. While you don't need to change who you are, you might want to take steps to get out of your shell and learn to be more comfortable around others so social interactions aren't as stressful.

One way to combat your shyness is to keep a positive attitude about yourself. Refrain from negative self-talk, such as "I'm not cool enough." You can also practice making and maintaining eye contact. At first, ask a friend to practice with you. Once you have these skills down, practice them on strangers. Go shopping and talk to salespeople. Talk to the teller at the bank or the clerk in the post office. The more you talk to people and the more often you make eye contact, the more comfortable you will become.

Tackle a Simple Project

You might not think of tackling a project as self-care. But sometimes checking something off a longstanding to-do list is very satisfying. To facilitate getting small projects done in your spare time, make a list of the little projects that need to be done around your home. Select uncomplicated jobs you've been wanting to tackle, but just haven't been able to find the time for. Here are some suggestions:

* Clean your desk or area where you store paperwork.
* Organize and clean an attic, garage, or basement.
* Go through that out-of-control linen closet or your grandmother's hope chest, or sort through a small drawer full of letters and papers.
* If a little bit of redecorating appeals to you, choose a color and paint one of the smaller rooms in your house.

Treat Your Brain to Chocolate

According to study results published in the American Chemical Society's *Journal of Agriculture and Food Chemistry*, cocoa powder has nearly twice the antioxidants as red wine and up to three times what is found in green tea. Based on the US Department of Agriculture/American Chemical Society's findings, dark chocolate tested the highest for antioxidants over other fruits and vegetables. Comparing the levels of antioxidants, dark chocolate came in with a score of 13,120; its closest competitor milk chocolate had levels of 6,740; and third was prunes at 5,770. The best source for healthy chocolate is raw, organic chocolate and the best outcome is to eat one or two small squares a few times a week, as it is, unfortunately, a tad fattening.

Notice Your Lies

It's one of our first life lessons. From the moment we come up with our first little white lie, we are taught that our word is sacred. However, as the years go by, telling the truth changes from an easily understood concept to a confusing notion rife with gray areas. Many people tell little white lies, half-truths, or useful falsehoods to evade blame, deceive others, deny reality, or to feel better about themselves. A little white lie, in some instances, might be motivated by a desire to prevent someone from being hurt.

The first step in breaking a habit of lying is to notice when you're doing it and why. Bring mindfulness to bear on the problem and you will find yourself more inclined to tell the truth. If you have lied, admit it to the person you've lied to. Then, take steps to change.

Set Aside One Hour for Crafts

After the day's chores are done, turn off the television and turn on your creativity. If you've got kids, great—they can join in as well. If you're working with kids, before choosing your craft, consider the ages of the children involved and base your choice on difficulty, safety, and any time constraints or short attention spans.

* Get crafty ideas online. Or you can visit a crafts store like Michael's for hands-on inspiration and to pick up the supplies you will need.
* Remember, the point of this activity is for everyone to have fun, so ignore the pictures of how the craft is supposed to turn out and have a good time.
* Use your imagination to let the craft take on your personality and preferences.

Celebrate an Unbirthday

Even if you haven't read *Alice's Adventures in Wonderland* (or seen a movie version), you may have heard of an un-birthday. It refers to the days of the year when it's not actually your birthday. The concept was invented by Lewis Carroll for his classic novel, and it's an idea that's gained popularity through the years. Celebrate your un-birthday today! It's a humorous and touching way to let someone know you care. As Carroll so wisely observed in his writing, an un-birthday can be just about anything you want it to be. Do you have a friend who needs cheering up? Or one who recently received a promotion at work? Celebrate in a new and quirky way by throwing an un-birthday party in her honor.

Set Out a Bowl of Freshly Crushed Lavender

Whenever you have a bad day, feel exasperated, and struggle to get out of a foul mood, use some lavender to restore your serenity. Lavender is one of aromatherapy's most popular scents. Scents like lavender, citrus, rose, and sandalwood can trigger particular memories or experiences associated with them. That's because your olfactory nerve carries the scent straight to your brain. Use freshly crushed flowers set out in a bowl, insert some reeds in a diffuser pot with lavender essential oil, light some lavender-scented candles, or put out some sachets of dried lavender. Allow the scent to lift your mood and remember that you never have to live a bad day over again.

Reduce Stress with Herbs

These days, herbal supplements are a popular tool for good health. Many people who cannot find relief for disease or pain through conventional medicine turn to an herbalist or other alternative-medicine practitioner for assistance. Frequently used herbs and natural remedies for common ailments include:

* Saint John's wort for depression
* Aloe vera gel for cuts and burns
* Cannabis (marijuana, pot) for pain relief
* Chamomile for sleeplessness and to reduce anxiety
* Echinacea for colds and sore throats, and to boost the immune system
* Ginger for nausea and motion sickness
* Parsley to aid digestion (yes, that's why parsley garnishes your plate)
* Peppermint for bad breath

Though the tradition of healing with herbs is ancient, the use of herbs for medicinal purposes has not been regulated by the Food and Drug Administration. Talk to your doctor before starting any herb regimen.

Have Dessert for Dinner

Have you ever gone to a restaurant just to get the dessert, but by the time you finished your entrée you were too stuffed for that sweetness? Well, try switching things up—treat yourself to your favorite dessert for the first course and don't leave room for dinner! This simple reward can help put that much-needed smile on your face at the end of a long day.

Avoid Conflicts and Confrontations Before Bed

Conflicts at bedtime can come about if one or both of you has not had time to decompress after work or if you have unresolved marital conflict. But when couples argue right before bed, it becomes virtually impossible to relax into restful sleep. Arguing before bed is unlikely to resolve the issue because you are both tired and not thinking as clearly as you will be after you've had a good night's sleep. Find a more appropriate time to have a healthy and constructive conversation about what's bugging you. Save bedtime as the time for love and rest.

Improve Your Memory with Herbal Remedies

As you age, the number of neurons, or nerve cells, in your brain naturally decreases, and you may notice changes in your short-term memory and other cognitive functions. Everyone can expect to develop some degree of age-related cognitive impairment, but you can help stave off the effects with herbal remedies such as:

* **GARLIC:** Aged extracts of garlic have been proven in numerous studies to reduce inflammation and cholesterol levels, which can contribute to the development of dementia.
* **GINKGO:** The best known of the cognition-boosting botanicals, ginkgo has proven antioxidant and anti-inflammatory actions and has been shown to fight normal age-related cognitive decline. Ginkgo has been shown to improve memory and attention in healthy young people too.
* **GRAPE:** Research has shown that extracts of grape seeds and skin can reduce age-related dementia and cognitive loss.

* **LEMON BALM:** Extracts of this herb, long revered for its ability to calm anxiety, have been shown to reduce symptoms of mild to moderate Alzheimer's disease.
* **ROOIBOS:** Research shows that this South African "tea" can offset the damage to the central nervous system caused by aging.
* **SAGE:** Sage extracts have been shown to improve cognitive function in people with mild to moderate Alzheimer's. Sage can also improve memory in younger people.
* **TURMERIC:** This aromatic South Asian spice contains a chemical called curcumin, which has been shown to inhibit the oxidation and other processes that are behind neurodegenerative diseases.

spirit

Reconnect with Your Spiritual Side

It's human nature to maintain connections that are important to us, such as with friends and family. If we lose that all-important connection, then we do what we can to get it back. When it comes to our spiritual side, we often don't make the same kind of effort. Losing our connection to our spirituality is much like the domino effect. We lose one thing, then another, and another until we get to a point where we feel drained and struggling to keep ourselves intact from the inside out. Make an effort to spend time reconnecting with your spiritual side. Rest, reflect, read spiritual writings, or talk with a spiritual adviser.

Understand How Karma Works

Karma is a far-reaching concept that has managed to filter into our society and into the everyday lives of even those who claim to have agnostic, indifferent, or atheist beliefs. It's an easy idea to accept and plant in even the deepest parts of our psyches. Even those who don't believe in reincarnation and in an afterlife of reward or punishment long to believe that the world around them is dictated by something other than chance or chaos.

The Sanskrit word "karma" comes from a root that means "to do or act." Karma is not punishment or revenge as many in Western civilization have come to believe, but simply a consequence of one's actions. Hindu philosophy maintains that every action and every thought has a consequence that will show up in a person's present life or in a succeeding one. You may not embrace all the tenets of Hindu philosophy, but owning your actions and recognizing that they have consequences is a critical step in developing a healthy, fulfilling spiritual life.

Celebrate New Beginnings

A new beginning is a wonderful gift. Unfortunately, that gift sometimes has to come out of a difficult period in our lives, such as divorce or losing a job. Some people prefer to use that time for personal reflection and would like to move on by themselves. For others, those can be the times when they need to know they have a support system of people who care about them. If nothing else, send your friend some flowers to show that you're thinking about her, that you care, and that you are there to support her. Some people might even be open to a party to celebrate a new beginning. No matter how exactly you celebrate, recognizing new beginnings can be a useful, even fun way of closing the door on one chapter and getting ready to open another.

Apologize to Someone

It is one of the hardest and most challenging things to do. But holding in those guilty or regretful thoughts weighs down your mind and soul like extra baggage that prohibits you from living life to its fullest. Admitting you are wrong and apologizing to someone will not only make both of you feel better, but it will also heal the past. Think of apologizing to someone as cleaning out that dirty attic that is getting dark and cluttered. If you are worried the words won't come out right, a handwritten note is the way to go.

Write a Thank-You Letter to Your Parent(s)

Take a moment today to write a quick note of thanks to your parents. It could be a letter expressing your love and gratitude for all their support over the years or a simple thank-you for the dinner they put on the table. It doesn't matter what age you are; it is important to thank them for their unconditional love. Try not to send this note on a birthday, anniversary, or holiday, but on a random day when it will take them by surprise. This note will fill their hearts and will remind them of what a good job they did raising you. Include a recent photo of yourself to personalize it.

Hug Three Different People

When we were little children, we got hugged all the time. As adults, we don't receive as many hugs as we should. Hug three different people today to get your daily dose of human touch. Many people are uncomfortable with touching someone else. These days, you can't just touch anyone—you might have a sexual harassment suit on your hands—so know who you are hugging and make sure you have permission. Studies have shown that just being touched reduces anxiety, slows heart rate, and speeds illness recovery. We've all felt or given a superficial hug: no real embrace and a quick pat on the back. Be mindful of that and give a real hug: both arms around the other person and a firm squeeze. At the end of the day, notice if you feel more relaxed than usual.

Find Answers in Your Spiritual Beliefs

When your heart is heavy because you cannot figure out the best solution to a problem, turn to your spiritual beliefs. To put your faith into practice, attend your favorite house of worship, be it a synagogue, church, temple, mosque, meeting house, or other type of place where you can find the answers you seek in an environment that provides a spiritual vibe. Then try the following three steps:

1. Think about the problem and give it over to a higher power, according to what you believe.
2. Ask for the answer to come to you as inspiration.
3. Then stop analyzing and let it go. Expect the answer to reveal itself in time.

Let Go of Anger

Holding on to anger, resentment, and hostility hurts you psychologically, emotionally, and physically. Don't give over your power to have positivity in your life just to harbor a grudge. You need to find a way to move past it. If you are holding on to anger or hurt instead of forgiving the person who violated you, you are limiting your capacity to feel good. Many great religious and spiritual traditions address the issue of forgiveness, reminding us that at our sacred center or core, we are inherently happy. Overcome that anger with these tips:

1. Whenever you slip into a place of pain and sadness, say a blessing for yourself.
2. Then say a blessing for the person who hurt you. Tell her (in your heart, if not out loud) that you will no longer take her or the memory of that incident any further into your life.
3. Then intentionally release the anger and hurt. Say an affirmation such as, "I release the anger I feel over this hurt."

Forgive, bless, and release. That's the way to keep your heart and mind open.

Understand the Law of Attraction

The law of attraction is based on the theory that we create our world through our thoughts and that what you focus on is what you get or create for yourself. Proponents of this law believe that if you go through life smiling, full of gratitude and recognition that life is abundant, you will act with honesty and generosity of spirit.

You can also use the law of attraction to draw to yourself the recognition you desire. Let's say the work you do is satisfying, but you want recognition for those big accomplishments and milestones.

1. Before you retire for the night, take five minutes to clear your mind.
2. Focus. Use your imagination to create a scenario in which you are receiving accolades, praise, and ovations by industry leaders, your business colleagues, and others.
3. Now, add your emotion to your imagined scene. Concentrate on your emotional feelings and mood as you listen to the words spoken by others about your achievements and accomplishments.

Set Personal Boundaries

If you are one of those people who has trouble establishing and enforcing personal boundaries, consider the power of the word "no." It has a purpose and place in every life. If you haven't established personal boundaries, people can take advantage of your kindness and you may unwittingly allow them to either use you or waste your time. When that happens, you get angry at them and perhaps also at yourself, and that's counterproductive—even damaging to your mental state. Ensure that you have firm personal boundaries in place and reinforce them with a "no" as necessary.

To put it into practice, decide on one personal boundary that you will implement immediately. For example, if someone is always interrupting you at work to chat, establish a boundary that the door to your office will be closed when you are working and that visitors need to knock first. Don't be discouraged if you find it difficult at first to establish your boundaries. You will become more skilled as time passes and you discover how much freedom and control can be gained by creating and executing a few personal boundaries.

Have a Séance

Connecting with our loved ones who have passed on is something almost everyone tries to do. We are naturally curious about what lies beyond this life: do we go to heaven? Do we watch and protect our friends and family? Do we reincarnate and start another life? We'll never actually know what happens, but it's good to be curious. Tonight, hire a medium to perform a séance for you and your friends. Ask everyone to bring an object that is somehow connected to someone they have lost. Keep an open mind and have fun. Accept any messages that come as signs of love from those on the other side.

Spend Time with a Sick Friend

Sometimes just spending time with a sick friend can help her heal faster. Your encouraging words and gentle touch can motivate and inspire her to stay positive and focused on the fight ahead. Try to avoid speaking about the activities she can't be involved in, but don't avoid reality too much, as she will feel as though you are holding back. Bring her favorite movie or game and spend a few hours with her. Although a quick visit is always appreciated, spending some real quality time will make you both feel better. Surprise her with her favorite snack, but check with her nurse or healthcare provider to make sure she's able to eat it. Find the best photo of the two of you and have it framed. Put it next to her so she knows you are always with her and rooting for her to get better.

Find Your Purpose

People who work to find meaning and purpose, and who live their lives making decisions and choices based on their purpose, are the people with the healthiest self-esteem. Finding your purpose is best explained by Parker Palmer as finding the thing that you cannot *not* do. That statement may sound somewhat abstract, but it means that you have found the talent, the passion, the miracle inside you that must come out. For some, it's music or medicine or repairing things or being around people. For others, it is surfing or writing or teaching or working with animals. It is sometimes described as "your calling." Living purposefully means that you have found your calling, your passion, and all of your efforts, desires, goals, and actions are directed by this purpose.

Learn to Trust Again

Learning to trust again after being betrayed is one of the most difficult aspects of being human. However, you should know that trust is essential for forgiveness and healing. It is essential for you to be able to move on. It is essential for healthy self-esteem.

Trust involves risk, and retrusting involves even greater risk. It means putting yourself "out there" again, sometimes with the same people who betrayed you in the first place. Trust is a self-fulfilling prophecy. If you let others know that you have full faith in them and trust them in earnest, they are less likely to betray that trust. Don't be afraid to say to a person, "I trust you completely. I have faith in you." The following steps can help you in restoring trust:

* Talk openly and honestly about your pain.
* Express your intentions to trust again.
* Start with something small and less significant.
* Be a person worthy of trust.
* Establish and communicate the ramifications of future betrayal.

Use Color in Meditation

Colors may be visualized in meditation for healing and maintaining certain states of mind. For this, select colors of matte board that can be cut into medium-sized pieces, either 8" × 10" or 9" × 12". Place the board in a quiet place without visual distractions. It should be to the right or left of your sitting area, but not in front of it. You want to be able to move your attention elsewhere if necessary. Look online for the meaning of certain colors and choose one that's right for your needs. Use one color per session.

1. Devote at least fifteen minutes to a color session. Give the overall subject a distant gaze for the first five minutes, then close your eyes. Look at the subject with attention to detail for the next five minutes, and then close your eyes. Gaze at the overall subject again for the last five minutes.

2. After the color visualization exercise, begin the color breathing exercise. Take slow, moderately deep breaths for five minutes. As you inhale, visualize the color on the easel lifting off and entering the body, circulating through it. As you exhale, the color fills the space around you. This may be done to "carry" the color's influence for a time.

Write a Letter to Your Favorite Teacher

It is never too late to thank that teacher who truly made a mark on your life. He may have been the one who constantly told you to stop chatting in class or the one who took the time to show you how to do your multiplication. Reflect today on that one teacher who changed your life and get his contact information. Send him a letter thanking him for all he gave you and how his teachings have made you the person you are today. If you graduated recently, buy him a sweatshirt with your college logo and send it to him. When your teacher receives this letter he will feel incredibly touched and inspired to keep educating others.

Have a Day of Compromise

Compromise is the key to a lasting relationship. Today, make a game out of it with your partner. Set an egg timer for an hour. Do something together that you want to do. Watch a favorite movie, go for a walk in the park, or take a nap. When the buzzer goes off, it's your partner's turn. Let her know she can pick whatever she wants: have sex, eat junk food, play cards . . . anything is fair game. You may find out that you didn't know what her true hobbies were.

Find a Long-Lost Friend

At one time or another, we have all wondered about that old friend from elementary school, high school, or college. We remember what he was like when we knew him and speculate on what he might be up to now. Until a few years ago, your best bet was to wait for the class reunion to arrive and hope to run into him. Thanks to the advent of social and career networking sites, you don't have to wait that long. Reconnecting with people you haven't heard from in years is easier than ever. Take time today to reach out to an old friend you haven't heard from in a while.

Learn about Another Religion

There are many religions in the world, but all seem to serve the same purpose. They offer comfort in times of need, answer important questions like "Where do we go when we die?" and offer us basic guidelines on how we should live our lives. Take some time to explore a religion whose history you aren't familiar with. You might be firm in your beliefs, but studying a different religion might open your mind to new ideas.

Forgive Someone

Today, take the time to let someone know that you forgive her. This isn't always an easy task, but forgiving someone for hurting you is important for your mind and body. When you hold on to grudges, you carry unwanted stress and anger. If you can't say, "I forgive you" in person, write a letter or just say it out loud to the universe. Find your own way to let it go. You will feel it in your heart when you do.

Discover More about Angels

You don't have to belong to a particular faith to believe in angels. They are a universal element of the unseen world and have been so since the beginning of recorded human history. When you feel the weight of the world upon your shoulders, seek out some angels and read more about them. Millions of people look to them as celestial companions that many of the religious traditions of the world have placed as intercessors between humans and a supreme being. Images of angels can be found everywhere. Their presence in art and literature can provide you with a source of strength and encouragement. You can also visit the Internet Movie Database (www.imdb.com) to find television series, movies, and documentaries about angels.

Tell Someone You Love Them

This can be either easy or hard, depending on if you've ever said those words to that person before. Saying it out loud can make you and the other person feel amazing, so it's worth it. Maybe you've been waiting to tell your new boyfriend or girlfriend your true feelings. Maybe you haven't told your mom or dad you love them in a while. If you were never close enough to your brother or sister to say the "L" word regularly, do it today. There is no time like the present, and everyone needs to hear "I love you." Say it loud and proud.

Find Comfort in Prayer

Whether you call it praying or taking a moment to reflect, remember to be thankful for the blessings in your life. Try to block out five or ten minutes every day—when you wake up or go to bed—to speak to your higher power. You may talk out loud in the car or rest silently in bed. Either way, take these moments to share your fears, hopes, and dreams. This daily activity will help you stay focused on your journey and keep you grounded. Try writing your prayers into a poem or song or drawing them as pictures. However you can best express your true feelings, allow them to shine every day.

Own Up to Your Mistakes

If you've made a mistake recently, an error no one is aware of yet, then act upon it immediately. No one likes to make mistakes, but when you've messed up, admit it right away. Though you might be afraid of taking the heat, accepting blame before anyone else realizes what's happened makes you look trustworthy and confident. Unless you've committed a major transgression, people are more likely to remember that you had the guts to come forward than they are to remember what you did wrong. And that can pay off for you in a big way in the long run.

Recite a Mantra

A mantra is a word or phrase you recite to clear your mind. Select a word or phrase with personal meaning to you, or one that is inspiring—such as "I am strong" or "I deserve love." Or you can recite a simple sound, such as "Om." Sit or rest comfortably, close your eyes, repeat the word or phrase, and focus on it so that all your other worries disappear. When you incorporate mantras into your daily life, you'll find that they help you feel empowered and reassured.

Laugh

A 2000 study at the University of Maryland Medical Center found that patients with heart disease were 40 percent less likely to laugh than those without heart disease. Cardiologists have found that hearty laughter actually improves the lining of blood vessels as well as lowers blood pressure and heart rate. In addition, laughter decreases stress levels and releases endorphins, which are the "happy chemicals" in your brain. Lighten up and enjoy life whenever you can.

Breathe Deeply

Take time every day to catch your breath, literally. Focusing on your breath not only lowers your heart rate and helps you refocus your mind, but it also feels good. Take a minute or so to focus on your own breath. Close your eyes and breathe as deeply and slowly as you can three times. In. Out. In. Out. In. Out.

Lie in the Light of the Full Moon

For centuries it has been believed that the full moon has a strange effect on human behavior. It has been blamed for violence, temporary insanity, insomnia, feelings of lust, and magical phenomena associated with werewolves. Some neo-pagans celebrate the full moon by holding rituals called esbats every month. It is seen as a very powerful time of the month. The next time the moon is full go outside on your porch or in your yard—wherever you can see the full moon clearly—and lie in the light of the full moon. If you have a telescope, look at the moon up close. Try to see if you feel any different by watching the full moon. If you start to howl . . . go back inside.

Meditate Before Bed

After a long day, your body, soul, and mind need a break before falling asleep. It is important to take some quiet time before putting yourself to bed to help calm all your senses and prepare for a good night's sleep. Light a candle, lie down, close your eyes, and think about absolutely nothing. Focus on relaxing each part of your body, from your toes to your head. Think of each muscle group letting go of all the tension and releasing the day's stress. You may want to end your meditation with a quick prayer of thanks for that day and hopes for the next one. Extinguish the candle and enjoy a peaceful night's rest.

Rid Yourself of Toxic Friendships

Friends help shape your self-esteem and friends aid in good health and long life. When you are in caring relationships, you are not lonely, and the less lonely you are, the longer you live and the better you feel about yourself. Unfortunately, countless people are in "friendships" to combat loneliness only to find that the relationships are abusive, controlling, and unhealthy. These friendships are called *toxic* or *contaminated*. Friends like this infect the way you act, think, and feel. They bring poison into your life and it takes a great deal of work to cleanse yourself of the debris. To assess your friendships, follow these steps:

1. Write down the names of your most significant friends.
2. Under each name, write down some of your most honest and heartfelt feelings about that person. How does this person make me feel? Act? Think?
3. Review what you wrote. You may discover that someone does not enrich your life and, in fact, may be a toxic or damaging influence.

Get a Warm Rose Oil Massage

A massage is a great way to release the stress and tension you hold in your body. There's nothing comparable to human touch coupled with aromatherapy to transport you into a place of relaxation and peace. If you don't like rose scent, ask the masseuse to use sandalwood, ylang ylang, myrrh, or your favorite essential oil. Massages are available at day spas and are sometimes offered at deeply discounted rates at local colleges with massage therapy training programs. Another option is to ask your significant other to give you a massage.

Live and Learn

Are you learning from your mistakes? You may view mistakes as embarrassing incidents that you'd like to forget, and certainly not as something you want to review and examine for potential life lessons! But if you're going to have a successful, rewarding life, you're going to have to learn that mistakes are an essential part of learning, and they're often the path to new and exciting opportunities. Spend some time looking at a recent mistake and understanding why and how it happened. You're not trying to place blame; you're trying to grow! But don't beat yourself up over the mistake. Learn what you can and move on.

Count Your Blessings

Get out a piece of paper today and count your blessings. Type them up, print them out, and cut out each one. Place them in a bowl and grab one every day just before you leave the house. On your way to work or on your lunch break, take a moment to reflect on that item. If you can, use that blessing to help inspire and motivate you to do something nice for someone else today.

Put Flowers on a Stranger's Grave

If you've ever been to a graveyard, you might have noticed that some gravestones have bouquets of flowers, flags, pictures, stuffed animals, and other trinkets, while other plots look like they haven't been cared for in years. Buy or pick a few flowers and choose a grave that looks like it needs TLC. It might seem strange to take care of a stranger's grave, but doing something kind for another person, even if she is no longer here, will make you feel good.

Donate to Your Favorite Charity

Giving back is one of the best ways to indulge yourself and those around you. By giving your money or time to a charity, you in turn feel a sense of humility and genuine pride in the work you are doing. Choose a local, national, or international charity where you would like to give your time or money on a regular basis. If you choose to give money to a charity, make an effort to attend their events to see where and how your money is being used to help those in the community. During the holidays, add a little bit more to your normal donation to show your spirit and gratitude.

Make Ethical Decisions

We all know stealing is wrong, but is it okay to take a few ink pens and a pack of Post-It notes home from work every week? Everyone seems to do it. Perhaps the most important word associated with ethics is "betrayal." Is there a worse word or act? Ethics demand that you consider this word. When you are making a decision, evaluating whether to act or not, or when you consider the consequences of a decision or act, is there any betrayal? If you have concerns about whether a decision you are about to make is ethical or not, or if how you have treated someone is ethical or not, consider the following guidelines:

* Will this decision hurt your reputation or the reputation of others?
* Is it legal?
* Have you considered every angle and option?
* Is it balanced and fair to others?
* Does your conscience approve?
* Have you betrayed anyone to make this decision?

These simple but important questions can help you learn to make ethical decisions. They can also help you build positive self-esteem, in that you know that you have done right by others.

Make a Ten-Point List of What's Important to You

Millions of people live their lives without a sense of direction. Unless you know what is really important to you and what you want out of life, how are you going to know where you are going, how to get what you want, and what your goals in life are? Think of ten things that are really important to you; for example, family unity. Then make each item as specific as possible. Instead of family unity, maybe you really mean eating meals together, working on the chores together, or praying together. Refine the ten things on your list until you know exactly what is of primary importance to you. These are the things that will make you happiest. Knowing what they are can help you take care of yourself.

Embrace Family Traditions

Most families have rituals unique to their family that they celebrate year after year. If your family is lacking in traditions, go ahead and create some! They don't have to be extravagant or elaborate. Brainstorm with your children and spouse about making a new family tradition. Perhaps something wonderful and spontaneous occurred as you were preparing to leave for summer vacation, the night before Thanksgiving, the afternoon of the first snowfall, or on the way to the pumpkin patch. Or maybe you had a pillow fight that ended with everyone making popcorn and s'mores and watching old movies in their pajamas. If it still evokes powerful memories for all of you, make it a tradition. Other ideas might include an annual family cleaning day (when everyone pitches in to tackle the mess in the garage, basement, or attic), an annual family fun day (let a child choose what the family does for the day, even if it's bug hunting), or an annual plant-a-garden day.

Keep a Dream Journal

Dream journaling is a method for managing everyday stresses that employs an underused part of your mind: your unconscious. For centuries people have speculated about what dreams really mean. Psychologist Carl Jung believed dreams express urges hidden deep within your unconscious. Jungian dream work views every character in a dream as a part of you, interacting with another part of yourself. Each dream, according to Jung, is a cry from your unconscious mind for change of some kind. Recording your dreams and studying possible meanings can be a fun way to learn about yourself. Whether you explore your dreams for fun or to communicate with your unconscious mind, dream therapy is another way to focus on your self-care by boosting self-awareness.

Watch the Sunrise and Sunset in One Day

Sunrises and sunsets are two beautiful experiences that occur every day. Today, wake up early, grab a cup of coffee, and find the perfect view so you can catch the sunrise. It will energize you for the day. The sunset will have a totally different feel, but will be just as gorgeous. We don't often take the time to notice these two events, but they are there every day for us to experience.

Hold the Door for Someone Behind You

Make an honest effort to hold the door for at least five strangers today. This simple courtesy sometimes feels as though it has been lost in our modern world. You may not always receive the proper thank-you or smile that you are looking for, but it will stay with them and may encourage them to do the same for the next stranger. Without even knowing it, you could create a wave of kindness that could have no end. Take a moment to selflessly hold the door, and hopefully it will come back to you one day.

Live with Integrity

Integrity is about doing what is right through thick and thin, day in and day out, year after year. An integrity plan is your personal mission statement. It is the statement by which you plan to live, act, treat others, and interact in the world. Having an integrity plan for your life is a declaration that guides you when things get dark and confusing. To create an integrity plan, make a list of the things that you value in your life. Your list may include things such as truth, honesty, fairness, spirituality, or friendship. After you have completed your list, you can begin to create a statement that incorporates your ideas for moral living, the things you value, and what you plan to do to protect your value system. It will have a forceful action verb to give the statement power, it will have objectives that guide you, and you will symbolically sign your name to this statement. An integrity statement might read something like this: "I believe in truth and fairness. In my actions, I will not do any deed that will jeopardize my integrity or the integrity of my friends. I will never compromise truth and fairness for personal or professional gain."

Practice Thoughtfulness

Being thoughtful makes other people *and* you feel good. To be sure you're a thoughtful partner, friend, and family member, remember these tips:

* Notice how you listen, how you speak; whether or not you thoughtfully choose your words or just utter whatever your mind is thinking.
* Do you ever remain silent or think about silence as the best response in certain situations? It often is, but many of us instead worry about "fixing" others' problems so we try to fill the space with words.
* Focus on only the person you're engaging with. Put away your phone and make eye contact. Ask follow-up questions.

Listen to Spiritual Music

The best music inspires everything that is good within each of us. It promotes dreaming, appreciation for expression, our own creative energy, and our reflections on all kinds of memories. You may not think you need more music in your life, but it should be clear to you that maintaining an adventurous perspective on the arts can keep you from stagnating and losing your enthusiasm for the pure pleasures of life. When you look into spiritual music, follow these guidelines:

1. Leave your reservations and feelings about the religion itself at the door. No matter what you personally believe, music with a strong, spiritual intent is that particular faith's idea of speaking to their creator in the most beautiful voice they possess.
2. Learn how different cultures and faiths speak to their creator. Your knowledge and appreciation of these musical devotions will make you a more intelligent, more productive citizen of the world.
3. Go to Amazon.com and listen to some samples of the diverse spiritual music from around the world. If something appeals to you, you can buy it to accompany you on your spiritual journey.

Do Something That Scares You

Being afraid of something can hold you back from making life-changing decisions or improving your character. How will you see the world if you are afraid to fly? How will you get that dream job if you are afraid to move? Facing your fear will boost your confidence and open new doors in your life. Today, make the choice to confront your fear head-on. If you are afraid of heights, take an elevator to the top of a skyscraper and look down. If you are afraid of water, ease your way into a pool or the ocean. Nothing should hold you back from accomplishing your dreams. Forget fear and move forward!

surroundings

Plant a Tree

Go to your local nursery today and pick out a nice tree for your yard. There are endless varieties of trees to choose from. There are evergreens, flowering trees, fruit trees, and ornamental trees, to name just a few. You can even buy a tree online and have it shipped to your front door. Check out www.arborday.org. You may decide to plant this tree in honor of someone who has passed away recently or even for a newborn in your family. It is a great story to tell when the child grows up and sees his tree, tall and proud, in front of him. You will not only add beauty and shade to your home, but you will also help improve the air quality, as trees remove carbon dioxide from the atmosphere. Get planting today!

People Watch

Go to your local park, mall, or town center and take a seat. Take some time to observe what humans do and say—it will definitely make you laugh! Try to listen to the conversations as people walk by. You will find great pleasure in hearing the snippets of peoples' lives, and even realize that we are all alike in many ways. You may find your single self viewing other singles as potential mates or just guessing what kind of underwear they are wearing. Some of the best things to see occur when people think no one is watching. You thought mature adults don't pick their noses? Think again!

Go on a Picnic

When's the last time your family went on a picnic? If you can't remember, or if the answer is "never," then you're missing out on a wonderful experience that can bring everyone together. Summer is the usual time for picnics, but you can certainly plan one during spring or fall if you keep an eye on the weather report and make sure everyone dresses appropriately.

To plan the perfect picnic:

* Involve everyone in the family from the start. Choose a date, then a location.
* Get everyone's input on the menu. You can stick with traditional favorites or indulge your adventurous side and try something new.
* You'll need a basket for the nonperishable items and a cooler for your drinks and for perishable foods.
* Finally, create the guest list.

Appreciate Your Surroundings

Even if you don't live in a cultural mecca, you can still appreciate all that your area has to offer. As you go through your ordinary day, stop occasionally and be mindful of what your community offers. Maybe it's a beautiful vista, or friendly neighbors. Maybe it's a thriving writers' community. Say a few words of gratitude—and think about ways to join in and support your community.

To really get a sense of what your town offers, be a tourist for a day or a weekend.

1. Plan your trip just like you would a visit to any community you don't know well.
2. Visit the website for your city or state with the attitude of a tourist looking for music festivals, art exhibits, and other cultural events.
3. Ask friends and locals what they recommend you see and do. You might be surprised to find all that your community offers that you never knew about.

Start a Book Club

Many of us have tried to go beyond simply enjoying a book by finding others who share an interest in literature. Some of us unfortunately have a hard time joining a book club already in progress—it can be difficult to just walk into somebody else's group and pick up as though you've been there the whole time.

Starting your own book club might be a better idea for you. Rally some friends or coworkers and set a date. Visit your local bookstore and ask a clerk what book he or she might recommend. Don't try to overplan or make it stressful—just bringing people together to enjoy a glass of wine and some lively discussion about the book you've read is enough to make a successful club.

Don't Use Electricity on Earth Day

Earth Day is April 22, and what better way to show the earth some love than by turning off all electricity for the day. Commit to unplugging all electrical items in your house. There will, of course, be the exception of the refrigerator and other needed items, but try as hard as you can to keep it minimal. Try using mass transit or riding your bike to work that day to help cut down on pollution. Whatever way you can cut back on energy use, do it on this day. This little bit of conservation will help the world, yourself, and many others to come. Check out your carbon footprint by visiting www.earthday.net.

Give Your Taxi to Someone Else

If you see someone else desperately trying to hail a cab right after you've gotten one, offer him yours. He may be in a rush and very grateful for your gift. Putting that positive energy out there will help boost your spirit and the spirits of those around you. This energy will have a domino effect throughout both of your days and inspire many others to reach out to a fellow human for the greater good.

Watch the Tides Change

One of the most amazing things that happen on earth every day is the changing of the tides. The tides are controlled by the gravitational pull of the moon; they go in and out a number of times during the day. Head down to the beach today to watch the tides change. You can check the newspaper or go online to read the tide charts, those handy daily updates that let you know when the tides go in and out. Bring a chair so you can sit right at the water's edge. The tides change slowly, so enjoy your time with your feet in the water.

Shovel Your Neighbor's Driveway

If you wake up to 10 inches of snow, take a look at your neighbor's house first. If she hasn't shoveled already, show some kindness and help her out. Look at it as a great workout! This act of love will not only surprise your neighbor and make her feel great, but it will also bring your neighborhood together. It is important to have a strong community where you live, and these random acts of kindness will eventually come back to you when you least expect it.

Pay for a Stranger's Meal

Plan to eat dinner out tonight. As you are enjoying your meal, look around the restaurant to choose another diner to surprise with a free meal. Do not wait for his bill to arrive. Explain to your server that you would like to pay for his meal. You can decide to pay anonymously or send your warm regards. He will be shocked yet pleased by this random act of kindness. On a smaller scale, you could pay for someone's coffee when you stop to grab yourself one.

Make Your Neighbor an Herb Box

If a new family is moving into the neighborhood, or you just want to thank a neighbor for letting you borrow their lawn mower or that cup of sugar, consider making them an herb box. You can pick up a flower box at your local hardware store. You can paint it or decorate it to match the colors of their house. Fill the box with potting soil and choose herbs you think they would enjoy. Plant parsley, sage, rosemary, and thyme, or perhaps some oregano and basil. Herb plants are inexpensive, and your neighbor will really appreciate the gift.

Participate in a Blood Drive

In light of terrible disasters that happen periodically, the importance of available blood has never been more important. Donating blood can benefit your local hospitals, but it can also aid the much larger community that exists beyond your own world. Don't wait for a blood drive to come to you. Check to see if there's a blood bank in your area. If you want to do even more, you can organize a blood drive of your own. A website such as www.mybloodyourblood.org can provide all the information you need. It offers advice on delegating responsibilities, finding a suitable location, delivering the blood after the drive has finished, and so much more. This may sound like a lot of work, but don't forget that you are making it possible for hospital staff and other healthcare professionals to give the gift of life.

Host an International Night

Persuading your friends to help you host an international night probably wouldn't be that hard. We love to learn about other cultures, and we often try to think of fun and unique ways to go about doing that. An international night can accomplish both. It's a good idea that lends itself well to a creative mind. Choose a culture you and your friends would like to explore—maybe a place you've always wanted to visit—and then go online for resources that will help make the experience authentic. Then try the following ideas:

1. Visit the local library and look for international cookbooks and books about customs, language, and clothing.
2. Download some appropriate music to listen to.
3. Encourage everyone to learn as much as they can before the party.
4. Then get together to demonstrate your knowledge and enjoy some fringe benefits like international cuisine or films.

You might learn some history, popular culture, language skills, and other things that stimulate conversation and create an atmosphere of discussion, education, and collaboration among you and your friends.

Start Birdwatching

Birdwatching doesn't necessarily involve a lot of time and work. All you have to do is walk by the window and happen to notice your feathered visitors. You can watch and enjoy them for a moment and then move on with your day. What matters is that you took a moment to let your mind move toward something more pleasant. Relaxing for even a few minutes can be a wonderful shot in the arm to a dreary day. If you want to find some binoculars, pull up a chair, and get more out of the experience, there's nothing wrong with that either.

You might decide to put up a birdfeeder or make your own birdhouse. A flock of birds enjoying the food and shelter you've left out for them is a soothing sight. If you're the kind of person who likes working with your hands, you're welcome to build your choice of house or feeder. But there's nothing wrong with buying something to draw those birds to your property. It could be elaborate enough to function as a nest or as simple as a small feeder.

Hit a Local Hiking Trail

If you enjoy working up a sweat, especially in nature, go for a hike. If your workday is just too long and there's no way you could do a hike in the evening before dinner, arrange to hike on the weekend. Get out early when the air is still cool and enjoy the fresh beginning of a new day. Plan to hike an hour or two along a local, scenic trail. Take plenty of water with you. If you love to take pictures or make notes about what you see, also slip your camera and a journal into your backpack. That way, if you see some breathtaking scenery or head off the path to explore the woods, you can document special discoveries along the way.

You can also participate in a hike organized by the Sierra Club or other local organization. Such hikes often have guides who can share insights as well as show you new trails. In addition, you can meet other trailblazers who share your interests in the rugged outdoors.

Find Shapes in the Clouds

If you are in need of some relaxation and want to enjoy the nice weather, lie down in the grass and take a look at the clouds. With a friend, create a game of who can point out the most shapes and objects. You may want to award more points for specific cartoon characters or animals as opposed to shapes and letters. Lying there and watching the clouds roll by can even whisk you away into a quick nap. This may seem juvenile, but allowing your brain to rest from the daily stress and focus your energy somewhere else can recharge your mind and give you motivation to get through the rest of the day.

Volunteer at a Nursing Home

There are many ways to volunteer your time at a nursing home. You can work for the activities department and play games like bingo or charades with the residents. You can show movies once a week and bring popcorn. You can paint nails or wash hair. Some residents might just need some company, someone to talk to. Many volunteers find it very rewarding to spend time with the elderly. Find out how you can help today. Even if it's just dropping off some cookies or donating large-print books, give your time and care when you can.

Make Your Home More Energy Efficient

Going green is all the rage, and so is saving hard-earned money. Do both, and make your home more energy efficient. Replace all of the light bulbs in your house with compact fluorescent light bulbs. They use one-fifth the energy of regular light bulbs, saving you a significant amount on your electricity bill each month. Remember to turn off the lights when you leave a room. Plug up drafts using door snakes and plastic on your windows in the winter. Invest in a programmable thermostat. With the energy you save, it will practically pay for itself. Taking these simple steps will make your home greener and your wallet happier.

Cook Dinner for Local Firefighters

Firefighters love to eat, but with their unpredictable schedules, finding time to cook while at work is hard. Tonight, make enough food for all of the firefighters on duty and bring it to your local fire station. They will love a hearty, home-cooked meal. Call in advance to see how much food you should make. A couple of pans of lasagna or a big pot of chili will feed a lot of people for a little money. If you don't want to take on the task by yourself, enlist the help of your neighbors to make a few dishes and bring them to the station together. Firefighters risk their lives every day to keep us safe; giving back is something we should all consider.

Grow a Vegetable Garden

Growing a vegetable garden is easier than it seems. Even if you have just a small piece of land, that's a great place to start. Till the soil so it is loose and free of large rocks. If you want to section off the space, lay some bricks or a wood border along the perimeter. You can buy seeds or plants that are just starting to grow from a home improvement or gardening store. Place them in a row and use markers that say what is planted in each spot so you remember. Each seed packet or plant should come with directions on when the best time to plant is and how much sun and water it should receive. In a few months, you will have wonderful, fresh, and all-natural vegetables. Share them with your friends or neighbors. At the end of the season, when you've put the garden to bed for the winter, continue to throw vegetable scraps into it. The seeds might bloom in the spring. It's like getting free veggies!

Have Lunch in the Park

Getting out of the office for a lunch break is one of the most important things to do during the day. You need to get away to recharge your battery and refocus, even if it's just for a thirty-minute lunch break. The quickest way to get some relaxation is to find a park that is close to work and have a picnic. Before you leave for work in the morning, or even the night before, pack a picnic basket with a lunch you can look forward to all day. A grilled chicken salad with baby spinach, strawberries, and blueberries is not only delicious, but also offers protein and important antioxidants. Remember to pack some healthy snacks that will give you a much-needed boost of energy during the second half of the day. Bring tangerines or clementines for a quick burst of energy and some toasted almonds or cashews for long-lasting energy. Don't forget to add something a little decadent, like a chocolate cupcake or a few oatmeal raisin cookies. Sit in the sun and close your eyes. Forget what you have to do when you get back to work; just enjoy your time away from the office. This is something you can do every day to treat yourself right.

Visit a Museum

Visiting a museum is fun and enjoyable to do with your friends, but if it's been a while or it's your first trip, it might be pleasant to go on your own. It's a delightful experience to spend time in a museum with absolutely no expectations. Visit the website for the American Alliance of Museums (www.aam-us.org) to find out everything you ever wanted to know about museums. With more than 17,500 museums in the United States, there's bound to be one near you that caters to one of your many interests. You might find something new to pique your curiosity, and if museums really appeal to you, there are plenty of volunteer and career opportunities available.

Go Horseback Riding

Most of us don't own our own horse, but that doesn't disqualify us from being able to enjoy the thrill of horseback riding. It might take a couple of tries to gain some confidence and skill, but once you start riding you might find it difficult, even impossible, to stop. It takes you away from the modern world and into a timeless place of indescribable freedom.

Imagine bundling up in a sweater and scarf on a chilly spring or fall morning and riding horseback along a beach past crashing waves or through a leafy forest glade, replete with dew-laden spider webs and small animals scurrying out of your path. The world looks and feels fresh and unspoiled from the back of a horse. It's a comprehensive workout that leaves you feeling accomplished and content, and the joy you feel observing the world from the back of a beautiful animal is beyond description. Visit www.horserentals.com to find a riding stable in your area. In the meantime, watch some riding videos on *YouTube* for some helpful tips and confidence boosters.

Adopt an Endangered Animal

With global warming posing a serious risk to the tropical rainforest and the polar ice caps, more and more animals are quickly becoming endangered. Through the World Wildlife Fund (WWF), you can adopt an endangered animal today. You can choose from hundreds of animals, like polar bears, penguins, blue whales, and toucans. WWF will send you a plush version of the animal you choose, an adoption certificate, and a photo of your animal. You can donate as much or as little as you want. If you decide to do this as a gift for your child, remind her that she doesn't get to take the animal home. Go to www.worldwildlife.org now to adopt your favorite animal.

Create a Scholarship in a Loved One's Name

Creating a scholarship to honor a loved one who has passed away is a wonderful gift, not only in honor of her memory but also for the student(s) who will benefit from it. The most important thing to do is raise funds for the scholarship. Donate your own funds or ask businesses in the area to donate. If your loved one was a member of community organizations or social circles, ask them to honor her memory by donating. You can even hold a fundraiser at one of her favorite restaurants. Next, choose a high school or college to work with so the scholarship goes to the best candidate. You may even be able to work with the school your loved one attended.

Feng Shui Your Home

Feng shui is the Chinese practice of configuring a space so that it is in harmony with spiritual forces. Feng shui enthusiasts believe that the arrangement of the furniture and objects in your home will help you achieve your goals. The placement of these objects affects the flow of chi, or life-force energy, in an environment, and using certain colors in certain rooms can affect the energy in your home. Do some research online to find out how to apply feng shui principles to the particular setup of your home.

Become a Big Brother or Big Sister

Are you ready to make a difference in a child's life? You can be that needed support that so many children are searching for. It's as simple as inquiring online and filling out an application. The organization will meet with you for an in-person interview to get an idea of what type of child you would like to mentor and to help make the right match. They will do a background check and ask for references to ensure the child's safety. Spending that quality time helping a child with homework or enjoying a sports event together will inspire and motivate her to do better. Visit www.bbbs.org for more information.

Join a Political Action Group

Are you dissatisfied with politicians? Do you hope for change? Do you hold a brighter vision for America and the world? Mahatma Gandhi once advised people to be the change that they wanted to see in the world. That means getting off the couch, turning off the television, and going out into the world and doing something to bring about that change. Join with others who feel as passionate as you about creating a more meaningful life and a better future through political action. Living and working toward a more meaningful and purpose-driven life is an important path to achieving happiness. Link up with other like-minded people. Make an effort to meet other politically active people by attending political rallies, working with charitable fundraisers, and joining environmental groups for hikes, birdwatching, or biking trips. When you join communities of like-minded people, you have more power to effect change, get laws enacted, and do good works.

Have a Yard Sale with Your Neighbors

If you want to clean house and make some extra cash but feel that you don't have enough to have your own yard sale, gather your neighbors together. Each of you should plan on posting fliers in different areas of town to help spread the word. Throw some burgers and hot dogs on the barbecue to feed those hungry shoppers. You may consider making this an annual event and get your whole neighborhood in on the fun. Avoid mixing your stuff with your neighbors' so dividing money doesn't become a problem.

Start a Babysitting Co-op with a Friend or Neighbor

If you can see that your neighbors or friends could use some couple time for a nice dinner or night out on the town, offer to babysit for free. These precious hours of alone time will allow them to think only about themselves and relish their relationship. Try to avoid calling them unless it is an emergency so they can enjoy the few hours they have. If you are babysitting for a toddler or infant, make sure you know all the dos and don'ts that Mom and Dad have put in place. Then, let them repay the favor so you can have a break with your partner.

Recycle

We hear every day how important it is to recycle, yet so many of us are too lazy to take a few extra minutes to follow through. In many towns and cities, recycling is mandated. By recycling, we drastically reduce the waste sent to landfills and decrease the amount of energy used in the production of new products. By taking these few extra moments in our day, we will make not only our world a better place, but the next generation's as well. Take a moment today to educate yourself on how to properly recycle in your home and set a plan in motion to become more eco-friendly. We must take care of our world, as it takes care of us. No excuses!

Go Camping

Camping can be incredibly fun and can teach you about mutual respect, responsibility, resilience, and survival strengths and weaknesses. Having the right gear and camping know-how can make the experience a lot more enjoyable. Talk with a professional at an outdoors store about where you'd like to camp and for how long. Make safety the top priority and discuss topics such as fire and water safety, wildlife encounters, getting lost, and avoiding noxious plants like poison ivy. Get travel maps and become familiar with park regulations before you head out.

Spending time in nature can draw you closer to see the wonder of creation and enable you to renew and recharge body and spirit.

Support Habitat for Humanity

Habitat for Humanity brings energy-efficient, affordable housing to the homeless of the world. Their incredible work is well-known, as are their most famous supporters— former President Jimmy Carter and his wife Rosalyn. Habitat is like any other nonprofit organization. They provide for people regardless of race or religion, and the army of volunteers comes from all walks of life. You can help your community by giving money to help build houses for your neighbors. If you'd rather offer your physical support, visit www.habitat.org to find out if there's an active build in your area and whether or not they're in need of volunteers.

Have Your House Blessed

Before moving into a new place is the best time for a house blessing, but it will still work if you've lived there for a while. Depending on your religion, you can have a priest or clergy member come to your home or you can even try it yourself. Get some sage to burn as you walk around the house and through every room. Burning sage cleanses the space of any negative energy. You can then go from room to room and say a prayer or just wish for happiness and peace while you live in the house.

Visit a Farm

You don't have to spend a month in the wilderness to get back to nature. Even a day trip to a local farm can put you back in touch with the good bounty of Mother Nature. Many farms are now offering tours of their facilities and a chance to buy the fruits of their labors. From fresh blackberries in the summer to crisp apples in the fall, you can spend some delicious time outside indulging in fresh produce—and still have lots to take home with you.

Create a Relaxation Room

Everyone needs a room in their house or apartment where they can just get away. This room isn't like your living room or bedroom; its specific purpose is for you to reflect or meditate, gather your thoughts, or just breathe. The most important aspect of the room is the ambiance. Use only candlelight, play some soft music, and burn incense if you like the smell of it. Paint the walls a soft color, like lavender or sea green. Use comfortable furniture like a papasan chair or even beanbags to sit in. Overstuffed pillows and soft blankets will make nice accents. Keep a journal or other creative materials there in case you feel inspired. If you live with another person or your family, you need your own personal space. Creating a relaxation room is the best way to have a space that's just for you.

Declutter Your Space

Every six months, go through your home and closets to see what you are not wearing or using anymore. Many of us keep clothes that we haven't worn in years and then end up throwing them out ten years later. If you no longer fit into something or you just don't use or like it anymore, let it go. Grab some bags or boxes, fill them, and find the nearest charity where you can donate, like the Salvation Army. In many cases you can fill out a donation form and deduct that contribution from your taxes at the end of the year.

Clean Out Your Purse or Wallet

Think of how much stuff you cram into your wallet or purse every day. Try to make this a quick, daily ritual when you arrive home from work. It will only take a few minutes to throw out the candy wrappers and receipts that you don't need. If you let this pile up, you will forget that gift card or important expense receipt you have left in there and may not find it until you are out of luck. You may want to create an envelope at home where you place all of your receipts to go through at a later time if it is too time consuming for every day. This quick and easy daily chore will give you a sense of peace knowing that everything is in its place and you are organized.

Buy Flowers for Every Room in Your Home

Fresh-cut flowers for every room in your house will not only smell wonderful, but they will also make each room feel special. Choose daisies or sunflowers for the kitchen— bright welcoming flowers for the most popular room in your house. Long-stemmed roses for the bedroom will add a bit of romance and elegance. A small bouquet of lilacs in the bathroom will be simple yet beautiful and smell lovely. If it is autumn, a vase of hearty mums can be a gorgeous centerpiece for the dining room table or coffee table in the living room. Choose your favorites, and if you can, pick wildflowers to save money. They will make you smile all year round.

Take a Sacred Labyrinth Walk

The purpose of a labyrinth walk is to provide an opportunity for you to clear your mind by focusing on a single task. You start at one point in the labyrinth and walk until you reach the center. This practice has been in use for thousands of years and is meant to give people a way to reach their own spiritual center. Walking the labyrinth can mean any number of things to any number of individuals. It's not specifically associated with any particular denomination of faith.

The website www.sacredwalk.com offers a basic description and links to literature, and it's probably your best place to start to learn more about labyrinth walks. When it comes to finding a walk in your area, *Google* should be able to point you in the right direction.

Watch a High School Play

It may have been a while since you were in high school, but a lot of things haven't changed very much. One thing that definitely hasn't changed is the fact that high schools often raise money through the production of plays and similar forms of entertainment. They promote their endeavors through the local paper, community bulletin boards, and especially on the large reader board standing in front of the school.

Show your support by attending a high school play. The kids don't have to be professionally trained Shakespearean actors to give a heartfelt performance. The important thing is that this is their Broadway, and by encouraging their passion, you might be nurturing a future star. Contact your local high school and ask about coming events, including talent shows, musical productions, and plays. Ask if you can help with any of the details of putting on the shows. If you want to be especially helpful, offer to do the jobs no one really wants to do but that have to be done—collect tickets at the door, show attendees to their seats, clean up afterward.

Maintain Your Neighborhood

In tough economic times, neighborhoods are facing the problem of blight: vacant lots, foreclosed houses, or abandoned property. They can become unsightly eyesores that drive down property values even further and make an area seem depressed and neglected. Get together with a few of your friends and spend a few hours doing some cosmetic yard work to maintain your neighborhood. Often, the owners of these properties are elderly or have lost their jobs and just can't keep up. Get permission from the owner (or, if you can't locate the owner, the city) before you do any type of work. You don't want someone calling the police on you while you're trying to do a good deed!

Warm Your Sheets Before You Go to Bed

Kramer from *Seinfeld* once used a pizza oven to warm his clothes before putting them on. This indulgence is a little less crazy, but just as comforting. Before going to bed, put your sheets and blankets in the dryer. When they are warm enough, quickly make your bed and jump in. You'll feel like you are in a warm cocoon and be out like a light in no time. Another version of this is throwing one soft blanket in the dryer before you sit down to watch a movie or read a book. It's sure to keep you warm in the winter or any time you are chilly.

sources

This book contains material adapted from the following titles published by Adams Media, an Imprint of Simon & Schuster, Inc.: *An Indulgence a Day* by Andrea Norville and Patrick Menton, copyright © 2009, ISBN 978-1-60550-152-9; *Happiest You Ever* by Meera Lester, Carolyn Dean, MD, ND, and Susan B. Townsend, copyright © 2012, ISBN 978-1-4405-3055-5; *Healthiest You Ever* by Meera Lester, Murdoc Khaleghi, MD, Susan Reynolds, and Brett Aved, copyright © 2012, ISBN 978-1-4405-3004-3; *The Everything® Giant Book of Juicing* by Teresa Kennedy, copyright © 2013, ISBN 978-1-4405-5785-9; *The Everything® Guide to Herbal Remedies* by Martha Schindler Connors with Larry Altshuler, MD, copyright © 2009, ISBN 978-1-59869-988-3; *The Everything® Guide to Stress Management* by Melissa Roberts, copyright © 2011, ISBN 978-1-4405-1087-8; and *The Complete Guide to Massage* by Mary Biancalana, MS, CMTPT, LMT, CPT, copyright © 2016, ISBN 978-1-4405-9401-4.